Z·U·L·U

Z·U·L·U

An Irish Journey

JOAN MATHIEU

—∞—

Farrar, Straus and Giroux • New York

Farrar, Straus and Giroux
19 Union Square West, New York 10003

Copyright © 1998 by Joan Mathieu
Distributed in Canada by Douglas & McIntyre Ltd.
Printed in the United States of America
Designed by Abby Kagan
First edition, 1998

Library of Congress Cataloging-in-Publication Data
Mathieu, Joan, 1964–
    Zulu : an Irish journey / Joan Mathieu.—1st ed.
        p.   cm.
    ISBN 0-374-29957-9 (cloth : alk. paper)
    1. Roscrea (Ireland)—Social life and customs.   2. Roscrea
(Ireland)—Emigration and immigration.   3. Mathieu, Joan, 1964–
— Journeys—Ireland.   4. Irish—New York (State)—New York.
5. Irish Americans—Travel—Ireland.   I. Title.
DA995.R57M38   1998
304.8'09419'2—dc21   97-37229

Earlier portions of this work have appeared in a different form in The Antioch
Review.

This book is for Virginia and Hilton Mathieu

*Special thanks go to Edward and Ann Marie Rich
for their generous hospitality.*

*But my deepest gratitude goes to my husband,
Benedict Hughes,
for his startling patience and support.*

Some of the names in this book have been changed as requested by those who crave whatever privacy is possible under these circumstances.

ROSCREA, COUNTY TIPPERARY

Ι<small>T HAD</small> been a sweltering European summer. Thunderclouds piled up all day until just before sunset, but at night the sky cleared up enough for radio waves. I was visiting family in Zurich for a few months after graduating from college. The whole time my thoughts, every word I read, and every road in Europe seemed to point toward Le Havre and the ship that eventually took me down the English Channel and across the Irish Sea. When I arrived in Roscrea (pronounced "ross kray"), County Tipperary—the town my grandmother Sarah emigrated from in 1912—my first thought was that my family must have always settled down in the places guidebooks warned us against, where seagulls came to scavenge when the lakes froze over, where oceans didn't reach, and where local history, if there was one, seemed undecided. We'd gone from one place to another with the same familiar horizons as if certain shrubbery and soils were binding from one generation to the next.

By living in one small town in central Ireland, I thought I'd discover who stays in these unreconciled parts of the world, and ultimately who leaves them. I was interested in Irish migration for personal reasons, but in the course of learning its specifics both in Roscrea and in New York City I would sometimes marvel generally at the results of migration and the diffusion of cultures across the world, ventures first recorded by the ancient Greeks in the days when people were classified according to where their shadows fell at noon. And I wondered if other migrations had confounded myth with history as much as the Irish had. Giorgio Joyce, the writer's son, used to call the Irish "zulus." Before I could even anticipate its appropriateness, this word began to appeal to me. It was in Zurich—between moth-hunting excursions in an Erlenbach ravine with my little niece—while reading biographies, rare reference works, and obsolete dictionaries that I kept finding it, until "zulu" became the strange term to fit the strangeness of the thing.

I traveled from Le Havre in steerage, which was like an upper cargo hold, an eight-foot-high space without portholes or ventilation, filled with five metal bunks and one sink. On the other side of the steel walls the engines, the pig-iron ballast, and water in the bilge shells clanged and splashed all night, but I'd managed to anesthetize myself against seasickness with black ale and antihistamines. Steerage was the one form of travel that most strongly connected the Old World to the New World and the one most closely associated with the history of immigrants, who traveled through one time zone after another, which sometimes took weeks with nothing but herring to eat. My trip took one long night in which I learned from a nautical dictionary that "zulu" was used in phonetic ship code in communications between different time zones.

By morning the ship had crossed St. George's Channel and landed on a stretch of wharves where nothing moved, not a bird's wing or a fishing boat. The fog was dense but lifting, and the dark smell of earth hit me with the first breeze. As I traveled west, impressions began to collect: furrows, hedges, and windows accumulating and darkening the fog, the simple black-and-white road signs joining one village to the next.

Near Bantry Bay I could still feel the boat rolling under my feet as images gathered around me—a copse of twisted oak trees with bark the color of Anglo-Saxon skin and the clarity of a Maxfield Parrish painting mingled with strawberry trees and an undergrowth of holly and profuse bryophyte flora and lichens. These oak trees once covered Europe's western upland and pushed mythology into the present long after they were gone themselves. When we were young, we thought Sarah ate chicken bones whole, this tiny woman who had left Ireland from Cork Harbor the same year the *Titanic* sank. By the end of the eighteenth century, 40 percent of those born in Ireland were living abroad. Between 1815 and 1914, over 30 million Europeans arrived in the United States, possibly the greatest shift in the human population ever recorded, although the U.S. government didn't start recording it until 1820. Of these, more than 4.5 million were Irish.

When immigrants landed at Ellis Island they were inspected for favus of the scalp, and their eyelids were lifted with a buttonhook, but, compared with incoming Slavs or Sicilians or any other kind of so-called low-grade immigrant, the Irish had an easier time of it. While still viewed as "alien filth," they usually had relatives waiting for them and spoke English, which made them more acceptable for domestic service.

Sarah spent six years in New York City before marrying an Irish-Canadian seaman. One day they boarded a west-bound train, thinking that they were about to become real Americans. In a book of railroad slang, I discovered that immigrants traveling west by rail were sometimes called "zulus."

SEPTEMBER

Built across the spine of a valley at the foot of the Slieve Bloom Mountains, Roscrea was destroyed by fire four times in the twelfth century, then continually rebuilt with what must have been a certain amount of skepticism.

One of the oldest towns in Ireland, with a population of 4,000 people and forty pubs, Roscrea held several schools, two banks, a handful of factories, and a relatively prospering, class-conscious society. Over the centuries it had become a watering hole to the stars—John Wayne, Maureen O'Hara, and Robert De Niro. But these streets were built for cattle, not actors; they were built for the exchange of produce and easy travel for landowners, each road connecting one shapeless town to the next. In the mornings the air smelled of vinegar and garbage tumbled from bins outside pubs. Some mornings heat from the sun rose off everything as if from a thawing lake. On Thursdays and Fridays there was such an urgent market tempo in the streets a traffic cop had to sort out cars. Like any Irish village, with all its fractured and migratory aspects, Roscrea was a microcosm of Ireland, if not the world, where outsiders were always outsiders and natives were never allowed to forget the street they were born on. The town seemed ready to sink back into the certainties of its past. The castle, built in 1280 at the center of town, had a gate tower, corner turrets, curtain walls with a drawbridge, and a museum all undergoing renovations. Some of the storefronts were being restored. Hammering echoed up and down streets on sunny days, wheelbarrows full of gravel sat across sidewalks; guide ropes left ghostly coils in the dry mud, and I knew that for years to come whenever I smelled hot tar I'd think of Roscrea. But despite the renovations, as far as I could see the town had managed to survive the plastic squalor of the last few decades. It had been built along winding inclines with smaller roads spidering out into the country, each house joined to the next, sharing one wall between them as if to form a barrier against change. But what came and went here—tourists, neon, polystyrene—seemed to me only incidental, barely making a dent across the town's deeper historical mantle.

The town's river had been a utility for so long that the architecture around it had acquired its own biotic forces. Moss covered everything in and around the river—walls, stones, and fist-sized rocks—and some said that the water occasionally ran red with blood from the meat factory. I called it "the river" because I wasn't sure what to call it. It entered town as the "Moneen," then swept under the Antigen Pharmaceutical Company, where, depending on whom you asked, it became the "Mall River" before changing into the "Bunnow" ("the bottom of the river") at the Catholic church, until finally passing the nursing home, where it then returned to the country.

The most intriguing road in town was a lane with bricked curbs and rows of white birch and cypress, forming a leafy tunnel with batik patches of light on sunny days. It was built by Roscreans in the late 1930s, without labor charges, to attract a meat-processing company. They built the road in six weeks, then put down their shovels and went to work in the factory when it opened.

———

We arrived the same day, the dead man and I, along the same road. I'd taken the bus from Dublin knowing only that Maureen O'Connor, a fourth cousin, had arranged "digs" for me. The bus windows were fogged inside and streaked with rain, so my only view was that of a nun across the aisle reading the Bible and chewing caramels.

Maureen O'Connor and her husband, John, lived on the road to Limerick in one of several town houses that lay along the basin of a hill. It had a tiny, walled-in garden of various plants including a broom shrub and flame-of-the-woods. Their house consisted of a tiny kitchen and bathroom (with a recently installed shower) just off a large main room and two bedrooms overhead. The walls of the main room, which was dominated by a large table that served for every meal, were covered with portraits and family photos of the last few decades—bell-bottoms, bouffants, sideburns. There were holy relics and an orange-eyed pheasant on top of a credenza, comfortable furniture, luminous lace curtains, unused china cups, and library books stacked up by the door. The room, with its warm, neutral fabrics and pale walls, looked as if it had been exposed to too much sunlight over the years. And there was a sort of erosion in the air, a feeling of children come and gone. It was a Friday. I walked here straight from the bus station and stayed all afternoon by the turf fire talking. A canary chirped in the kitchen.

"At night the ashes keep the embers from going out altogether," Maureen said, which made her fire about fifty years old. She had a dark, placid face, almost Mediterranean, and a serene levelheaded approach to the world, always waiting for something, looking out the window, moving through the house, and setting the table in slow essential movements without ever offering or expecting empty gestures.

The idea that I might walk the short distance across town to the cold-water rooming house she'd found for me was out of the question, so while Maureen arranged a ride for later in the day, John, a lanky, good-spirited man with a long, hardened face and a horse trainer's constant look of stern appraisal, showed me his aviary of songbirds in the cement yard in the back. There were dozens of them in all colors, stacked up in cages in a shed. He also showed me his antique pots and field tools painted a thick black and artistically arranged against the whitewashed side of the shed. His two grouchy, overfed corgis whined behind a gate and crows circled above a confusion of clotheslines on the other side of the wall. Although he was recovering from throat cancer and had trouble talking, John teased me about the "lads" and Guinness. Most of the day he read the regional newspapers, finishing a section, then handing it to Maureen, who folded it and put it under the cushions of the couch without a word.

Maureen had a habit of biting her lower lip when she smiled that reminded me of my grandmother. When I was young I'd been afraid to walk by Sarah. She always had something to say and expected a sharp reply. My sisters and I believed a trunk in her basement was filled with the bones of dim-witted children. No doubt she found our jumpiness tiresome. She once threatened to cut my sister's tongue out with a pair of scissors, and it wasn't until we were adults that we realized she'd been teasing. In fact, she'd been by turns affectionate, playful, and callous, and what she admired most in others was something she often lacked—compassion. She died before I was ever able to have a real conversation with her, but I remembered her asides to me about Irish summers and dancing in New York City, an old woman reminiscing.

Maureen couldn't remember much about the young Sarah, just that she'd been the fifth of eight children, most of whom emigrated to England. Of those who went to America, one returned almost immediately, one died there, and Sarah, who stayed, did not return to Roscrea until seventy years passed and, for reasons I had yet to learn, long after her mother, Mary O'Reilly, was dead and buried. Sarah had been "the spoiled one," which meant that, unlike her sisters, she'd been allowed to bring her boyfriends to the house. The person I should talk to, Maureen insisted, was Chris Kearnes, Sarah's niece.

Maureen and I continued talking, by the end of the day

covering more general topics—politics, disease, and Protestants.

"When I was fourteen," Maureen said, "the nuns and the priests punished me for looking at a Protestant wedding in St. Cronan's there. I don't know what came over me. A grand white wedding, i' twas. I'd never seen such a sight in all my life, and I'll never forget it. At the time you could not go to confession if you'd so much as walked into a Protestant church; you'd need a dispensation from the bishop himself if you did. But that's all changed now, thank God. I remember another time, a Protestant man, in a fit of rage bashed down a streetful of festival decorations with his walking stick. Just went around bashing everything. A Catholic festival, i' twas." She thought some more and, growing more exasperated with each memory, added, "When we met the priest we knew to get off the path, genuflect, and bless ourselves. Isn't that terrible? We have the ecumenical service now, and isn't it lovely too?"

She tucked her hands into her sleeves and looked at her shoes, then out the window. On the wall, above John's chair, there was a glamour photo of her, very young with long brown leather gloves, a chic hat, and the same patient, watchful look in her eyes.

Under the picture window looking out to the street, which was as busy as a highway, a television flickered at us silently. Throughout the afternoon we would glance at it, occasionally trying to figure out what was happening in the world. We talked about the United States and family.

Maureen's sister Margaret—a jolly, cryptic woman—joined us from across the street. I took photos of the two of

them along the garden wall while they primped and protested.

"She's raising holy hell with that camera."

"Will you stop."

"You'll never leave, Joan."

"Yes, we'll have you married before you know it."

"Let's find her a rich one. Don't go for that charm; that
soon runs out," Maureen said, giving John a significant look,
which he ignored.

I'd just finished up a roll of film when Margaret said,
"You arrived the same day, the dead man and you, along
the same road." She nodded and folded her hands together.
" 'Twould do you some good, so." She nodded again, punc-
tuating certain words with her head. "You'll see, there's
nothing like it. Everybody says so. You'll go then, you
will."

I looked at Maureen, but she was looking intently into
the distance. Her legs were no good, she said; she would not
be going.

"At eight o'clock," Margaret continued, "and he'll be
buried in the morning, so." Finally I understood: Margaret
had just invited me to someone's funeral, someone who was
not a relative of mine.

"It'd be a way of introducing you around. Everyone will
be there."

Margaret went back across the street, and the day passed.
Maureen made bacon, cabbage, potatoes, and lemonade, and
around seven-thirty Margaret and I headed out. She was a
round little woman with blue eyes and seagull-colored hair,
walking with her arms folded across her stomach. We
headed east toward the church, around a hairpin corner

down Limerick Road. The blue sky between chimneys had filled gradually with the afterimages of the darkening streets below. The air smelled of humus, and turf smoke clung along the rooftops, not as insistent or as rich as a campfire's, but a humic coal that you smelled more with your heart than your nose.

Along the way, Margaret spoke to everyone we met, mostly women in flower-print dresses.

"Mrs. Maguire, near the graveyard there, she found some money in the street. Thirteen pounds."

"Did she? She left her umbrella behind at my place. She found thirteen pounds, did she?"

"Yes, that's right. I'm only after talking to her."

"She has osty."

"I have rheumatoid. I buy sandals I can't wear them."

"Even Cuban heels?"

"I'm only after hearing from Mrs. Meagher. She's crippled with arthritis too."

Just before reaching the "new" church, which had been built in the 1800s, we passed the crumbling remains of a fifteenth-century Franciscan monastery. Its bell tower and a section of the choir and the nave still stood, surrounded by an iron fence, walls covered in vines and moss and set deep into the Paleozoic earth with stones sagging one layer into the next.

I heard a spade being dug into soil and ivy snapping off a wall somewhere in the shadows of the tombstones. The river with three names ran through the cemetery, and the tombstones spread up a steep hill, looking beige and small like braille in the weak light.

We walked across a bridge and entered the church. Inside, the pink of the Caen marble and the delicate triforms dominated the altar; above it a host of gold angels stretched their arms toward the pews, and along the side there were windows depicting various scenes and popular saints, rich dark wood carvings and bead glass—the fourteen Stations of the Cross, images created, like the Sistine Chapel, to instruct the illiterate. Cold radiators lined the pews, and the Virgin Mary looked down on a table of whale-oil candles with the face of a goddess. It was all familiar to me, the metaphors of the church still holding, although losing force and complexity. Everywhere else the church had become less like a house of God and more like a museum, but here people still genuflected to the ground and invoked St. Anthony of Padua for a lost set of keys.

The church was packed with men lined up against the back wall. There was no music or singing. The funeral cortege entered at eight o'clock behind the priest, a red-faced, porcine man, shaking the sleeves of his soutane so abruptly that his clip-on microphone screeched with feedback. Otherwise you could hear no sound except that of trousers brushing together as the pallbearers moved toward the high altar, the tapered pine coffin across their arms. The priest's faulty microphone gave his eulogy a horrible eloquence, one word booming out at a time, "blood . . . beg . . . sorrow."

The prayers for the dead began slowly, invocations receiving almost blasé responses at first but growing louder, more urgent until they became a prolonged cacophony. Then, without warning, it ended. I felt I'd missed something, the silence was so abrupt. Margaret tugged my arm as everyone crowded up to the front pews at once, and she whispered, "Now you say, 'Sorry for your troubles.'"

Jerry Mahir had been an emigrant, twenty-eight, when he died.

———

The annual average influx of Irish immigrants to the States reached 34,000 between 1986 and 1990. It was said that those left behind suffered economic, psychological, and cultural strain and that those returning to Ireland were gradually eroding the old ways here and leaving a population of the very young and the very old. So I felt lucky to be living with four young women about my age. Most migrated to Roscrea to find work. They were all engaged to be married or nearly engaged, and sexual intrigue loomed over the weekends. Anne, the only Roscrea native, worked the swing shift at the ribbon factory and a couple of nights at a gas station. Kate and Margaret worked time and a half at the Antigen Pharmaceutical Company. Kate, the daughter of a mortician with "loads" of money, was a bright young woman with an intense curiosity; her hair hung in her face and she often cocked her head to see around it. Margaret was idiosyncratic, intense, and always distracted; she never stopped moving or talking. She told me Antigen had been set up in the late 1940s to develop a cure for pernicious anemia. The company had a clean, modern design straddling the river. They worked long hours in lab coats and surgical gloves. If any of us were sick or couldn't sleep, they'd get us samples of antibiotics and codeine—our own Valley of the Dolls.

Maisie taught at the convent, a quiet girl, who spent her evenings smoking in front of the fireplace, filling one ashtray after another. When I arrived they questioned and cajoled me as if I were a sparrow fallen in the fireplace.

"When we heard a Yank was coming we were so excited."

"But we'll be honest with you—we thought you'd be a busty blonde with matching luggage."

"And we decided to tell you the loo was out back and pigs lived in the kitchen . . . but you're not what we expected."

"You're quite normal. We're very disappointed altogether. You look Jewish. Are you so?"

"Don't be a fucking eejit," Anne said. "Of course she's not Jewish." Rail-thin, pretty, with long blond hair and always suppressing a grin, Anne took me under her motherly wing.

"First, you've got to learn to keep yourself warm," she told me. "Now, this is the range. Don't let it go out if you can help it."

She lifted the round iron lid off with a metal hook, knocked the cold ashes from the night before with a gnarled walking stick through the grill to the trap below, which she dumped in bins in the alley. When she came inside her hands were smudged gray and a breeze had sent a flurry of ash across her jeans.

"Manky yoke," she muttered, which meant something like "dirty thing."

Next she made a pile of new turf, lighting the machine-pressed bricks with fire lighters (like Styrofoam soaked in kerosene), then piled the rougher slabs of turf on top (with the grass and roots of last spring still snared in their cracks) to keep the fire going.

"Look there." She pointed at a copper flue along the wall. "The heat moves along that yoke. Your room, now, that'll be the coldest. I'm only warning you like, but you'll be all right. Now what sort of heating do they have over there in America?" she asked, hands on her hips.

I admitted that all I knew was that a vent blew hot air and hot water poured from the tap with the "H" on it.

"You're very stupid," she informed me but in a tone that suggested this could be fixed.

———

Although I had spent most of the first weekend sleeping, I managed to fill a kitchen cupboard with tea, butter, sugar, and brown bread supplied by Maureen O'Connor. At one point the range began to smoke the kitchen, so Anne threw the back door open.

Saturday afternoon I rented a manual typewriter and stopped to see Chris Kearnes, as Maureen had suggested. Chris was Sarah's niece, a cheerful eighty-six-year-old woman who was as wrinkled and dark as a tree.

"Welcome home, sister," she said to me. Chris and I shared an interest in Mary O'Reilly, who was Sarah's mother, Chris's grandmother, and my great-grandmother.

Unfortunately—at least for now—Chris's key interest seemed to be in keeping Mary O'Reilly a secret, just as Sarah had done. In fact, the first time I asked Chris about Mary O'Reilly she just laughed and changed the subject. "See that chap across the street? He started wearing shorts to protest women wearing pants."

I walked back home, remembering that whenever Sarah walked down the street she spoke at length to almost everyone she met, asking blunt if not audacious questions, in turn resisting any inquiry into her own life. Even as a child I knew there had to be more to her past and her homeland than a late-setting sun.

Sunday night I kept waking up out of dreams of burning buildings. But by Monday morning a warm light filtered through a radiant fog. I got dressed while the kettle boiled for tea, then went to a corner garage to rent a bicycle. Apparently no one had rented a bike in Roscrea in years, so the garage owner seemed a little wary before finally handing a three-speed over to me, and as I cycled toward some unreachable-looking mountains, my head began to clear at last of jet lag and burning rooms.

It was only after getting out in the country that I began to really perceive Roscrea's intimacy with its surroundings and the dual aspects of the Irish landscape itself. First of all, it's an enormous park, a land stripped mostly by glacial changes and partially by England's industrial engine. What was left—the demesne, folding valleys and rolling swards of grass—seemed more hospitable to humans than animals. But it was its second aspect, the drenched wintry ground of the bog, that took a stronger hold of me. It seemed to magnetize the air around it with its odd and multifarious flora. Hundreds of bodies had been discovered across Europe, embedded and refrigerated in the remains of coal forests. The moss that grew over the bog and held the water in its spongy leaves also blocked oxygen and gave off a bacteria-killing acid. So bodies emerged from time to time, making the front page in more marginal publications. I thought of the Tollund man, a well-preserved Iron Age man, sacrificed thousands of years ago and retained to this day. He was discovered in Denmark in the 1950s, which reminded me of the young emigrant and his abrupt funeral. He also died in Denmark.

A dog barked and I realized how alone I was out here. There were a few farmhouses, sheep here and there, and some cows. But it was as if the ghost of some struggle had driven everyone else inside.

I turned the bike around and headed back, this time noticing various signs of neglect—a row of unoccupied and decaying houses, a distillery ruin—all of it reminding me that I was here to find some direct and personal basis for this abandonment. Instinctually I looked back as I pedaled into town to make sure that ivy and moss weren't swallowing the road behind me. And I thought of the Tollund man keeping the secrets of his day in his mixture of toluol and paraffin in a central Jutland museum and the young emigrant buried in drift soil along a river with three names.

———

Emigration is a sacred right in Ireland. But I realized that for years I had never considered Irish immigration a diaspora in the usual sense. In school I'd looked at these gray, somber-looking projection maps with arrows crisscrossing the planet, making the same spiral paths of insects toward light. My mother visited Roscrea when I was about ten; and still the diaspora from places like the Maghreb or Gabon or El Salvador had nothing to do with me or the T-shirt my mother gave me when she returned from her three-week vacation.

The fire had gone out and a wind was howling down the chimney, so—because I hadn't yet mastered the range—I went to the library, a modern brick building just a few yards from us. Inside, everything was small, like a children's library, but it seemed well run. The head librarian and I talked for a moment about overrated writers. I checked out the complete works of Oscar Wilde, and she promised to get me so-called objectionable material, which was code for books that weren't banned per se but couldn't be put on the shelves. More secrets. Before leaving I noticed an interesting piece of art on top of the card catalogue called "The Leper," a polished wood carving in a mixture of rich shades of crimson and ivory and scarlet. I knew that before the disease was eliminated in Europe and other parts of the world by the Great Plagues, old leprosy remedies ranged from arsenic in China to turtle soup in Portugal, but I wondered what meaning a leper could have in a small Irish town where its old leprosy remedy—whiskey—still thrived.

———

One day I had lunch in a drafty little tea shop with Sinead Kirwan, a bright, chatty twenty-two-year-old with a wholesomely rural face and big bright eyes. She was clerking at a store where I bought my newspapers when we met. She wore a sweater, jeans with heavy stitching, and stylish boots. I imagined a bedroom full of stuffed toys and music posters, but she also seemed to be a little bit edgy, perhaps too chatty, as if some self-awareness or the shock of borrowed time were breaking through. At the end of November, she was going to emigrate to the States for the second time. The first time she left, her mother begged her to come back, so she did.

She had been educated at the local convent girls' school.

"They're solid. They give you good manners, and an emphasis on deportment, and it was a school that listened to you, but the middle class are not given a fair run at the system. You either have to be extremely intelligent or have a lot of money to go to college. Look, I'll give you an example of what it's like. In Dublin . . . Dublin, mind you, for people like me, a tourism information desk job is considered highly valued and is very competitive."

She fell silent, then after a moment added, "It makes you bitter. I worked at the Offray ribbon factory. After three months, when pay review came up, they let me go." She'd been working as a secretary for an accountant, but when he told her to start cleaning the toilets, she quit. I asked her about Ireland's notoriously heavy welfare spending.

"The government system encourages people not to work. People only work out of pride. In fact, there's a joke going around . . . 'I'll buy the drinks; you're working.' But the dole's not for me this time. I want to see more of life. All my friends have left and I have cousins in the Bronx, my home away from home. I'll waitress and be a nanny. America really is the land of opportunity although they look at us as being backward."

Sinead's home away from home was part of a typical emigration pattern in which a chain of friends and family saturated one area and formed a close-knit homogeneous community, turning New York neighborhoods into urban villages. Although Ellis Island closed as a port of entry in the 1950s, New York still attracted more immigrants than any other U.S. city. Illegal immigration was rampant and uncontrollable, with 2 or 3 million from all over the world quietly filtering into the States. For the Irish, the usual plan was to go to the States, work hard, and save a lot of money in a few years, then come home, not that it always worked out this way. Sinead knew the ropes; she'd sneak away behind her mother's back to avoid an emotional scene. On the plane she'd "dose" herself with Bacardi rum. On employment forms she'd describe herself as a student, give a false social security number, and expect half pay under the table.

"The lifeblood of the country is missing and they're surprised if you stay around this town," she said finally. That afternoon I kept thinking of something Sinead had said in anticipation of her plane ride: "I'll watch the green land go away," as if it would not be Sinead leaving Ireland but Ireland leaving Sinead.

———

A week or so later I took the "back road" out of town about a mile west, where the air smelled of the treacle used in a mill out this way, along wooded demesnes, rookeries, and thick green fields. The sky in the east turned black with clouds, and the sun, which had broken through on and off for the last hour, was still shining chalky cuneiform shapes across the edges of the valley. My cousin Thomas Kearnes, Chris's son, had worked at the Fanure Fish Farm for twenty years. I came out here to ask him about Mary O'Reilly, having become more certain that she was the agent behind Sarah's decision to emigrate.

When I arrived Thomas was counting thousands of fish ova in the black water of two incubator bins. The light was dim in the fertilization shed, and the eggs were the color of Mars. He looked up—"How are ye?"—then lost count and started over, his lips moving.

His clothes hung shapelessly over his bony frame, and he looked like a dust bowl farmer with his weathered but unassuming face, curly brown hair flattened against his head in oily rings, an effortless grin, and a dark glow that brought to mind certain Flemish Renaissance portraits.

He was born in 1943 to poor, uneducated parents. His father was an exceptionally quiet man who'd been sent here from a Wicklow orphanage to work in the meat factory. A journeyman carpenter most of his life, he'd been dead now for five years.

The Kearneses lived on a lane called Bohreenglas in a house with one main room, three bedrooms, and an open fireplace, living mostly on snared rabbits and fish. Of the ten children, Thomas watched five die, one by one, with pneumonia and meningitis, the children laid out on the kitchen table in their best clothes.

"You would see the steam rising off their foreheads."

As a boy Thomas played along the railroad track, and hunted rabbits and crow's nests. To get into the circus for free he'd put circus posters up around town. He cut turf and went to dart matches with his father. School didn't interest him; in fact, instead of memorizing multiplication tables he memorized rebel songs.

His surviving sisters (two of which still lived in town, two in England) taught him to dance, and in the winter they played dice and gin rummy, read movie magazines, and listened to Bobby Darin records.

After quitting school at fourteen, he took various jobs: at a pub he sorted corks in boiling water, then washed and labeled forty dozen bottles of porter a day; for two years he filled ampules at the Antigen Pharmaceutical Company; for five years he worked as a gardener at the convent. When he started earning £100 a week as a meat trimmer at the meat plant, he bought a Morris Minor and kept himself in good clothes. When he was offered a chauffeur's position with a Guinness heiress, and a chance to travel the Continent, he turned it down, "knocking the chance" for the sake of a woman he did not marry.

Eventually, he took a job at the Fanure Fish Farm. The fertilization shed was connected to a government building, which contained science labs and hallways flaking an aqua-colored paint that looked committee-chosen forty years ago. Woodland and marsh surrounded the whole farm. The river ran first into two ponds where herons, cormorants, and swans fed on the banks. Further south the river turned back into a utility again, channeling water into rectangular breeding troughs full of rainbow and brown trout, bringing in oxygen and carrying out waste.

"I like the job I'm doing because I'm producing something with life."

A few years after he started work at the fish farm the economy fell in on itself.

"The 1970s destroyed us all. There was an awful lot of money stirring and everything was at its height. There was no end to it. When it hit the 1980s, people couldn't cope without the luxuries, but the incentive to work had been killed."

One weekend he met a woman on a train and married her, he said, "for her honesty alone." They'd been married eighteen years.

I waited for Thomas to finish counting the fish ova, then we walked around the fish farm, its moldering buildings and tanks submerged in the weather and dark greenness surrounding it. He carried a bag of feed for the fish and gave me a handful to throw. Where the pellets fell, the fish rose and created spiral graphs across the water's surface.

"The people who lived here before were very well off, but they were unlucky. Alcoholism and suicide brought an end to them. This place is haunted. Do you see this marker?" He pointed to the remains of a stone shed where a worn inscription seemed minutes from eroding away altogether. "A man was kicked to death by his own horse in 85 A.D."

Thomas walked with a slight limp due to back pain, he said, from playing too much golf. He swam regularly, but he still didn't have the country club vigor of any American counterpart. He had instead a resigned composure in the face of a changing world. He'd come of age during an economic boom in the 1960s. Things were different. Emigration had never tempted him, and America didn't interest him as anything other than a threat to world peace. At first something kept me from asking him about Mary O'Reilly. I kept imagining an alternate life for Thomas, the life he might have had somewhere else. But of course this was pointless. When I asked him what he'd do if he won the lottery he said, "Destroy myself."

Despite the neglect of the buildings the twenty acres of land were still beautiful, bounded by various streams and filled with chestnut trees, holly bushes, and a fir tree Thomas called the "monkey puzzler" because of its multitude of branches. A fading apple orchard lay at the edge of the property where the soil was soft and gray. Leaf pieces flickered in the winds, and the air smelled of ants and the coming rain. Thomas looked at his watch—which seemed to be a way of getting rid of me—then picked up a small bumpy apple for the pony.

When he began working at the hatchery, there had been twelve other men. Now there were just two. The others had taken early retirement, found other work, or gone on the dole (or both) in the economy's downward spin.

So he worked seven days a week with few, if any, vacation days, and when he did take time off, he cut turf and took odd jobs plastering, plumbing, and wiring. But he seemed resigned to this hard work and talked about it with no bitterness in his voice.

"I think it's very unfair that a person who is unemployed can be equally or better off than a person who's working. I've seen people giving up work, they're on the dole, and they have a medical card; I have no medical card. They've free travel for the kids; I've no free travel. They have fuel vouchers; I have no fuel vouchers. They have free hospital fees; they've everything. I'm working at a hundred fifty pounds a week. I have four kids, my wife is due with the baby, and I've no benefits except my own dental insurance."

Again, he looked at his watch. The sun skimmed behind the clouds and thunder rumbled close by; it seemed to come from the roots of the trees.

He suddenly pointed toward the far side of the pond along some brush shrubs; a heron stood preening itself.

"They're murder on the fish." He retrieved a rifle while I waited. "Lord, Joan, cover your ears." He fired and missed; the heron flew over the trees. He leaned the rifle against his hip and shook his head. Thunder rumbled again, and as we instinctively stepped away from the water, I finally asked him about Mary O'Reilly. Thomas stopped and stood with one hand on his hip, looking down at the gravel where large raindrops had begun to splay out. After a moment, he said, "She was a bag o' cats, Joan. That's all I know." Then, as awkwardly as checking his watch, he changed the subject.

"This place is full of ghosts," he said. "Would you believe that? That's God's truth. Sure, but you wouldn't believe it if I told you, Joan. I've heard the ghost of a woman and her child, me and some of the lads. You can ask them, if you like. Coming from the hallway up there by the science laboratories. They come and go, a woman and a child with her. Their voices."

———

I was having doubts about what I was doing, digging into the history of someone so opposed to it, and maybe it was guilt that propelled me. But a few days after talking to Thomas I started walking along the road out of Roscrea, then cut west across Munster toward the Atlantic Ocean. It was warm. Grass clung in masses to the ground. The fog, this fugitive anatomy holding the glacial terrain together—the slow rivers and smooth, low hills—finally cleared by midmorning. By then, with the rain splitting gullies into feeders, the roads held the weakest light imaginable.

Mile after mile, the land divided into traveled and un-traveled roads, while in front of me the landscape spread out into layers of Klimt greens, auburn, and purple in deep mo-rainal gloom. The matrix of fields grew less and less ordered with each acre toward the west. Because there had been less tenantry toward the Atlantic, the land evolved this way from east to west, from large, ordered spaces with ditches and hedges to small chaotic fields surrounded by low stone walls.

In trying to appraise the land, it broke me apart limb by limb with a crack that began in the soles of my shoes and became holes that widened with every hour. It took me four-teen hours to learn this. Water collected in my socks and turned each foot the color and texture of a monkey's paw.

The West of Ireland had always been the most deeply affected by emigration. In 1841, Ireland's population was over 8 million people. Ten years later it dropped to 6.5 million because of famine and emigration. Deprived of farm-land and food, the country began to empty out, filling ships, sometimes 500 people in spaces meant for 150. In those days a third died on the way. In the West especially it created an appreciation for land—where you lived—and education— the thing that took you the farthest away from it.

Following river drainage patterns, I half expected the ocean to suddenly loom through a valley and stay there for hours before me, shimmering gloriously across the horizon, but instead I kept reaching the point when everything just seemed too far away—Moneygall, Nenagh, Ennis—these towns which had little to their names; they were just cross-roads feeding rural life. I didn't see a lot of people, which was due, I supposed, first to nineteenth-century famine, then to a scarcity of minerals worth exploiting for large-scale industry. There weren't many houses along the way either, just endless fields, the human population and number of softwood trees dwindling at about the same rate. But the difference was that the lack of trees seemed unnatural whereas the lack of people felt as though some global law of distribution was being strictly followed.

I stuck my thumb out for lifts and received a few from men and women who had varied qualities neither country nor city, their faces clouded by curiosity, never going much farther than the next crossroads, with never enough time for much conversation. I also saw a lot of junk that day— crumbs, sandwich bags, car floors covered with papers the color of drying leaves, rust and handle knobs coming off in my hand. Everyone smoked.

A farmer with protruding eyes gave me "thumbing" advice, delivering each secret slowly with minutes passing between them.

"Look the driver in the eye . . . Don't lean on anything: that makes you seem lazy . . . Always stand on the far side of town but not too far out, otherwise cars is going too fast like."

One man with a long open face and curly hair—and a wisdom cribbed from song lyrics—told me that Tom Wolfe was a genius and that my mentioning James Joyce made me an elitist.

I kept walking kilometer after kilometer, moving closer and closer toward this weird topography of sinkholes and caves, where the rivers ran underground. If you scratch a certain kind of limestone and spit on it, it will fizzle and corrode right there in your hand. On a large scale this was the area of County Clare called the Burren or "great rock." There was no pattern in its corrosion, except what grew in the thin soil between cracks, the saxifrages, gentians, and mountain avens; but on the rock and in the region around it, human patterns registered that much more strongly through surrender and music, isolation and anger. Entire cities had been lifted out of these houses.

Lisdoonvarna, a place recommended by guidebooks, was near the ocean though not near enough to redeem the town's weasel intensity. Old men in foulards and captain hats giggled into telephones. Others in moth-eaten sweaters and buttonless cuffs sat alone, looking around in open despair, plying their ears with keys, cleaning teeth with penknives. Bumper stickers proclaimed "It's great craic" ("craic": Gaelic for "fun"). With an American western-style main street, long wooden ramadas, saloon-type lobbies, and "grand" hotels featuring sulfurous spring baths for those who wished to "take the waters," the town seemed more like a setting for early American hucksterism.

The patterns that began here and echoed the region's past were that of something spinning down, of traces left behind by a force as capable of damage as it was of beauty. And it seemed that nowhere else would I see so clearly how a nation goes the way of an ice age.

I stayed in a hostel. Early in the evening, as I waited for a clean blanket to be found, I had a drink at the bar and talked with a man who had recently returned from Saudi Arabia. He had big ears and thin curly hair and an effusive, comic manner. Raised by several sisters, he was a genial, self-proclaimed "women lover." He informed me that Lisdoonvarna was in the middle of a matchmaking festival.

"If you as a woman talk to them," he said, eager to dissect the mental condition of these sorry-looking bachelor farmers, "they'll look in your ear, the way your hand rests on your face. They won't believe what they're looking at, and if you turned to them and asked, 'Where's the dance?' they'd never forget it for as long as they lived. Never."

It was clear that, because of internal migration, there were too few women in rural areas and too many in the cities. As recently as 1945, one-quarter of Ireland's farmers were still bachelors at seventy, but the man added that as an American I would not be expected to understand this. He drank and pointed toward my pint, indicating that I should do the same. I asked him if he'd ever been married.

"Oh, aye, but I've since gotten what you'd call an Irish divorce." At the time divorce was illegal; an "Irish divorce" meant he had no legal or financial obligations to the family he left behind.

———

The next morning was dazzling and cold, chilled by the first ground frost of the year. After a breakfast of strong tea and strawberry scones, I walked about six more miles, descending a coastal plain and reaching the ocean along the furthest edge of a flat rock bay with fissures big enough to hold a car. The seas around Ireland were shallow; they mingled tidal currents and rivers of plankton, which attracted the fish and seabirds, and, further up the food chain, the tourists. The three Aran Islands, just eight miles off the coast, were an extension of this land, where sections of bleak rock were carpeted with small ossified tundra plants and algae colonies. There was a sense of finality and recklessness along this coastline, and I did nothing as the day progressed but sit on a rock. Silver reflectors scattered over the waves like thousands of invitations from the Gulf of Mexico.

The dark sandstone cliff of Moher rose up from the water to the south where peregrines and rock doves nested, and the breeze carried the smells of wet dog and sour weeds. Skinny boys in cutoff jeans smoked and threw rocks into the water. There was a fat man in a wheelchair, his legs wrapped in a red plaid sea blanket, who had an enormous black patch over his right eye. A few yards from him an old man, wearing nothing but white underwear, crouched among the boulders staring deeply into the seaweed fronds and silky green rocks below. He didn't move for at least two hours; in fact, every time I looked he was crouched there, the knobs of his backbone turning gray.

Usually the wind off the water blew a tropical warmth transported in the salt of the Gulf Stream across the land, but that day the wind still felt chilly; on the concrete pier old men huddled together at the south end of the bay waiting in suits so old and worn they seemed to have sprouted on them thread by thread—but waiting for what? Lobsters waved at them from cages. Toward late afternoon a drunken, rowdy group of sightseers began to gather along the pier to wait for the trawler that would take them to Inisheer island. Then, just before sunset a young woman in a violet bathing suit dove off the pier, her skin turning the color of cabbage underwater. Everyone on the pier seemed to hold their breath with her, waiting for her to emerge from the icy green water to a smattering of applause.

"She's great for the water," one old man said to all of us.

She did wonders for the water, I thought. I myself had no plans and certainly no energy to do anything, much less to keep walking north to Galway, or anywhere else. The water eased my misgivings, perhaps because oceans have always proposed a means of escape, dating back to the ancient Greeks, who were habitual migrants. I decided to join the crowd and get on the boat. It never occurred to me during my several hours on the rock to question why I'd just walked across Ireland in the rain or why now I was picturing myself gliding across the water to reach some raw perimeter of Europe. But I recognized the impulse. Tourists want to see the familiar distorted; they want to make the dramatic transition and connect with what has been severed. The causes for emigration had been so various and persistent throughout history that Ireland had become, not just for the Irish, a symbol of natural demographics blown off course. But more than anything, we came here because we wanted to see the rain make this grim terrain shine.

I bought a ticket.

On the boat I met an elderly couple from Ohio, with perfect manners and a sort of Presbyterian clarity, who reminisced about meals they'd eaten the world over. Here, they'd be visiting cemeteries and reading in unison from brochures. Inisheer boasts a prehistoric fortress and the remains of an eleventh-century Romanesque oratory. They gallantly ignored the drunks and the fact that, with the boat chopping wildly across otherwise tame waves, our captain too seemed to be on the second or third day of a really brutal drinking jag. They continued reading in unison: The islanders live in dry-stone houses, relying mostly on tourism for a living, and, as on the mainland, migration and emigration are the norm.

When we landed, a red sun was setting just over the gray dome of the island rockscape, and the smells of flint dust and turf hung in the air. There were a few osier trees, but Inisheer consisted mostly of black outcrops, flat vaults of limestone, and tiny man-made fields fenced off by heavy oblong rocks stacked up in layers, crisscrossing the island in winding labyrinthine patterns like some primeval communiqué with the gods. But that was exactly it. It seemed the islanders didn't want to speak to landlocked mortals. They were polite and generous, but they ignored us as if to create a barrier, not just to protect themselves but to reduce us to one impulse between them and the outside world. On the mainland, Irish (which sounded to me like a thorny combination of French and Hebrew) was all but a ghost language. A New York bookdealer had told me Japanese businessmen were buying up Irish dictionaries with an avidity that seemed to portend the death of the language. English had been so successfully adopted in Ireland because it was the language of economics and emigrant relatives. Here on the island, however, Irish was their first language, and it alone kept us on a separate standing; it alone made us feel like ghosts.

After a dinner of boiled chicken, I went to a pub—that cherished but, for female journalists traveling alone, usually frustrating ground. Looking sobered and sour, the same group from the boat stood along the bar, trying vainly to recapture their sense of adventure. There were no velvet cushions or brass railings here, just chairs and tables and a splintery wood floor. Galway language students played a set of Irish tunes and Don McLean's "American Pie." I spoke to some local fishermen at the table next to mine, a group of bright-eyed men in decorously woven sweaters who would not have looked out of place in a Harvard Square cafe. Although their English was very good, my questions about migration seemed to puzzle them. They were anxious instead to discuss their favorite TV show, *MacGyver*, which was, as I recalled, hokey but harmless enough: an expert government agent who could, for example, make a bomb from a lightbulb. This was what seemed to impress these men who risked their lives every day fishing from the sea in currachs made of canvas and tar, but who didn't know how to swim. Swimming to them just delayed certain drowning; it would not be one wave, they believed, but the whole ocean that would get them.

So we listened to the music and talked a little more, but I was never able to get them off the subject of television. I suppose in a way they saw me as one of those "MacGyver people," whispering our wild rumors of the twentieth century; and television, which should have formed some kind of alliance between cultures, only warped it, numbed their curiosity about me, and made communication impossible. As I was leaving, they asked me if I knew J. R. Ewing.

The sun had been down for hours on this stony knot of an island. I walked around in the darkness for a while. As if through a heavy shroud, I saw the faintest bone-gray strip of the beach, scarcely paler than the water or rocks around it. I dimly saw the white foam of the waves breaking on the sand, and there was an opaqueness of sound, which must have been a steady wind in my ears. The golden-hued Saturn sat south between the horizon and its zenith, and Neptune, buried in the stars of a centaur, sat somewhere in the east. Seventy-seven years ago that week—possibly that very night—a sixty-pound meteorite had landed in County Limerick in a shower of stones. It would have had the same spectral signature as all other pieces of rock that don't have the gravitational energy to stick together, that break away from themselves. This one fell in 1913, the same year lightning struck Roscrea's Catholic church.

—∿∿—

The next day I found myself once again on the mainland after an uneventful ten hours of retracing my steps back across this igneous land. Thorns ground together in the wind like little wooden teeth. (Some people said that hawthorn flowers still carried the odors of the Great Plagues.) I reached the Shannon's sprawling banks and the wide dusty avenues of Limerick—also known as Stab City—its streets teeming with shoe stores and pubs.

I checked into a hotel room with a credit card and, although exhausted, went out again, as if driven away by the color television and bathtub in my room, these modest luxuries that at the moment were a little too alien for me. I walked the streets, which were empty; dust blew up from the sidewalks. I'd been remembering the clay salt maps we used to make in grade school, the purpose of which had been, I supposed, to give us some vigorous, tactile sense of the earth's character and our place on it.

I heard singing from a pub and went in, settling down at the bar with a couple of newspapers. Almost immediately the singing stopped, and the group turned away from the piano to stare at me. At the count of five the baritone, a tall middle-aged man with a bushy mustache and an assembly-line slouch, came over and started telling me jokes. His friend, a tenor, an older man with white hair and an unhealthy red face, soon joined in.

"What do you call a donkey's grave? An asshole."

"What is the height of confusion? The height of confusion is Father's Day in Killarney."

The baritone had recently returned from England.

"They didn't like me over there. I'm Irish; I stood up for myself. But I know people in America, now. Sure, all of my school chums moved to New York. I like Americans," he continued. "They're kind of part of Ireland. We built America, you know."

"The Italians helped, the Chinese helped," I added, I thought, reasonably.

"Bastards," he sputtered.

I wasn't sure if he meant the Chinese or the Italians, but it was here that the evening seemed to rotate and float to the surface.

"I saw a documentary on the American Indian," the red-faced tenor said. "I love the Indians. Now, they built New York City, did you know that? Because no white man would climb the beams of those skyscrapers. The Indians were fearless." His legs grappled momentarily with the floor. "They were cheated."

I agreed with him, but he kept insisting, as if we were locked in some bitter dispute. I was an American, he reminded me, and as such I couldn't begin to understand.

—⁓—

I took the train bound for Roscrea, feeling tired, my bones thawing out, too edgy to sleep. Banks of pale grass rushed by as I pondered the compiled lists and charts that go into the descent of a single person. And family trees. In school, I decorated mine with lumberjacks, cabdrivers, cooks, recluses, and runaways until the tree became lopsided before vanishing into an empty page; I had to believe that my family sprang, not from an ocean, but from nowhere.

I was suspicious of this convention, basically because the children who drew the lustrous, monolithic trees seemed to be the more virtuous, especially when their branches, like graceful, sturdy oaks, stretched as far back as the *Mayflower*. *They* received the gold star; the rest of us were left with stunted bonsai.

And I understood the branchless nature of obscure, even hidden family histories. I'd been hearing the silence of it in conversations around Roscrea, and I felt their resistance as they tried—with good intentions, I'm sure—to protect the tree. There was no way I could convince them of the tree's irrelevance to me; I wanted flesh and blood. But I wondered if the resistance was mine. My first few days in Roscrea I'd met briefly with a few other distant cousins. I remember standing in an unlit room full of men and boys. They seemed strangely primitive, as if they'd never experienced even the mildest female influence. They took out this enormous family tree—this thing that they treasured and what looked to me like a meaningless circuitry of names and dates—and unfolded and folded it with the greatest delicacy, as if it were a scale diagram of heaven. When I looked at this immense, incomprehensible object, I decided I wanted to keep my own page empty and concentrate on the tangible.

The train creaked and wavered around a bend.

I took out two photographs of my great-grandfather and great-grandmother, Richard and Mary O'Reilly, these two who have presided over my life like childhood crimes. There was something very familiar about them, but I didn't know what. I searched each face, marveling narcissistically over the cheekbones, the skin, the sharp lips, the bony foreheads, and wide jaws, this levee of features about to break across several generations into what was known in our family as the "Mitchell look"—like a startled, angry bird. We all crave the story of ourselves so that we can measure our successes or, when necessary, feel ruined by them.

Richard was a tailor. I'm sure he made his own suit and that the camera, and not some strength of character, shaped his posture. But because I'd always traced my family along the more vibrant matriarchal line, Mary interested me more. She was a woman of habit rather than vice, I would say, but who knew? That kind of information might disease the tree.

Their hands were more expressive than their faces. Richard's fingers curled in while the thumb and index finger extended out, which made me believe that he smoked a pipe, that perhaps he'd been thinking about that pipe and about the tobacco pouch that was sitting in his coat pocket. The first phalange of his index finger was swollen, the finger of a man who wore a thimble all day for thirty years. Mary's fingers on her right hand curled into a loose fist, and I wondered if she might have been hiding the turf dust in her nails, if she hated her life, and if she was a bitter woman who maintained bitter thoughts. (In Hebrew her Christian name, Mary, means "bitter.")

I imagined they both ground their teeth in their sleep. But still, I found nothing in those features to explain my affinity to them. I wondered about the room they posed in and the light around them. Was the carpet at their feet pocked with burns from a fireplace? Was someone boiling a chicken in the next room? Could they hear the creaking bedsprings of two people making love overhead?

I had to believe that it was the light more than anything, and not the "Mitchell look," that struck this familiar chord. Out the train window it was one of those days with a flat consistent light that left me tense and aimless and produced shadows like those in the photographs. My day would end in total darkness; ultimately these photos were only the settings for uncelebrated lives, and as if staring west across an ocean, I found no explanation in the water or in the photos for why their daughter Sarah (which in Hebrew means "a princess") became an "exile."

Sarah's relationships with her own six daughters had been rocky, but she always encouraged them to leave home. Perhaps recalling her own origins, she told them, "There is nothing around here for young people."

———

The Sacred Heart convent school was an enormous mausoleum of a building overlooking the cemetery and the Catholic church. To reach it the students walked through Rosemary Square up a steep hill along the wall of the priest's manse, but I preferred to reach it along the summit of the cemetery where the groundskeeper burned leaves and the nuns were buried. From this approach the place didn't tower over me so much, and I could see the way its fjords of old stone adjoined lime blocks and wood annexes, reminding me of an inner-city hospital, with each addition reflecting every fiscal rise and decline; it had been taking on new shapes ever since Sarah attended as a girl. Inside, the sunny hallways smelled of lemon floor wax and institution soap. Handheld bells rang each hour and the girls waded through the hallways in packs, their lives mysteriously thrilling.

The principal, a lively no-nonsense nun with a dry handshake, showed me around. One teacher took me aside to tell me that the convent would close in about five years and that schools would be "amalgamated." She uttered this word as if repeating someone else's obscenity. "Boys and girls together." I walked up to the top floor, where from the library windows the town looked like a stony enclosure under bluish-brown smoke and fog as if under murky water.

In one class they learned about plagues and famine. In another they learned that the protagonist in *Catcher in the Rye* was Holden Caulfield. And back downstairs in the teacher's lounge they talked about AIDS.

"Teach them the Ten Commandments? That's horseshit," one man said. "I might as well be a vegetable." It hit me that in the time it took me to descend a few flights of stairs I'd spanned two centuries, from the physical and social plagues that sent thousands away, to the plague that some were returning with.

———

Unlike animals that migrate—birds, spiders, squids— humans don't always make the wisest choices. As he admitted himself, Anthony Maher did not survive well outside of Ireland. I met with Anthony and his wife, Peggy, one night in a pub with deep velvet banquettes, oak paneling, and a fireplace that gave the place a Teutonic energy. On the television high up in one corner a Las Vegas singer kept riding up and down in an elevator. We stepped through the crowd; when Anthony introduced me to a stonecutter— "the only genius in Roscrea"—the stonecutter grew sullen and turned away. Anthony giggled and patted him on the back.

I received a few stares as I ordered a pint instead of the more acceptably ladylike glass of Guinness, then Anthony and I sat down at a small round table in the back of the pub while Peggy stood along the wall talking to a friend. Peggy, a shy woman with small, frail features, said little to me and kept her coat on, arms crossed. She looked as if she might be recovering from a long fever as she sipped a glass of "sparkling glucose."

Anthony, on the other hand, reminded me of the pa-terfamilias in a French novel who gives orders and forgives no one. He wore a silk foulard and gold glimmered in his teeth. Bald on top, with a Roman nose and unyielding green eyes, he had a grave energy, always leaning forward as if bent on turning the mildest remark into some personal, ter-rible truth, his grin part malice, part mischief. And there were mysterious streaks of gray dust on his sweater. This was the convent's art teacher, the man who thought the Ten Commandments were "horseshit."

Born in 1947, Anthony was one of nine children raised under a crumbling pretext of wealth in clothes provided by aunts and uncles living abroad.

"It was a question of rural pride. No one was supposed to know where your new coat came from."

His mother had been intelligent and musical, but his father was a contentious, miserly, and austere Catholic who believed arguments should be resolved with boxing gloves. He and Anthony would go years without speaking to one another.

"It was a good life but hard; they were strict. I was milking cows when I was three years old."

At sixteen, he sailed to Australia by way of Gibraltar, Naples, Alexandria, and Port Said.

"Some bastard there tried to sell me some sexual stimulant; I didn't know what in Christ he was talking about. That'll show you what kind of eejit I was. I spent a week in Bombay, which will stay with me the rest of my life. People dead in the streets black with flies. And I saw what people had to do to make a living. In order to get a few shillings one woman with a small baby would take the child's two legs in her hands and throw her up in the air, twist her around and catch her again. It was dreadful."

By the time he reached Queensland, Munster idioms had become obsolete and the symbols of the Old Testament distorted.

"Adventure is fine if you're equipped for it. Most are not."

For seven months he woke at three o'clock in the morning to hunt kangaroo and dingo on horseback, repair dams and windmills, and castrate lambs. You castrate lambs with your teeth, he explained, because it's faster and there's less blood that way. He loved Australia. But, in the end, he became homesick, and after losing seventy pounds, grew deathly ill before finally coming home.

"I think those who come back are disappointed in themselves. I worked on the farm shoveling shit in order to send my younger brothers and sisters to university, which was a normal thing to do." One brother ended up going to Canada, another to Australia, and one sister wound up in the Sinai Desert. Anthony studied antiques and art collecting, and at twenty-one, being "good to draw," he went to the Limerick School of Art, working in mine fields digging mercury and copper to earn tuition.

We sat in silence for a moment, sipping Guinness and watching the crowd. Anthony's father had died a few weeks earlier.

"Seven priests stood over his grave," he said abruptly, "and I sat there totally mesmerized and thought: What in the name of Christ are these people doing? The bloody man is dead. He's a box of bones and flesh, and they make a circus out of it. It's nothing got to do with religion." He quietly but theatrically beat the table with a half-opened fist, every word spoken with glinting clarity, every "t" crackling.

"Religion's got more to do with tradition in this country than anything else. My father, in his piety and hypocrisy, turned me against religion and for that I thank him. Fuck the priests as far as I'm concerned."

He grinned, a look of slightly unbalanced good humor in his eyes. He glanced around the pub for a moment as if he suspected that a petition for his death was being circulated, then drank, nearly polishing off the entire pint in two gulps. He leaned toward me. "There's a man who comes here. He usually stands over there." He pointed with his chin toward the bar. "I hope to see him in a wheelchair. I want to see him die like a pig in the ground. This guy is the secretion of an adder. There aren't words in the English dictionary to describe this man's character and everybody in Roscrea knows it. Do you know what it's like to be wronged here?" He pointed to his chest.

Peggy was still standing along the wall, her Lucozade evaporating. Anthony got up to fetch us another pint and to briefly console her. When he returned he plunked down the pints, then grinned at me as if the pub itself was the object of some shared joke. By now it was well past closing time; someone stood vigil by the door, looking for gardaí (the police) as people slipped out one at a time, but quite a few remained. "Time now, ladies and gentlemen, if you will," the publican called over the heads at the bar. Everyone ignored him. Anthony and I glanced up at the TV: the Las Vegas singer now looking worried.

Anthony, a man who was that much more firmly rooted to this land because he'd once left it, drank hurriedly and then beckoned Peggy over. "Nice to meet you," she said to me, relieved to be going. She invited me to come out to the house sometime and they said goodbye and made their way through the closing-time crowd.

"Time now, please," the publican begged the rest of us to go home.

———

It may have been just a question of misbegotten demographics, but there was a lot of death in Roscrea. One day I attended the death vigil of a distant relative. She lay in the upstairs bedroom of a low-income housing estate dying of cancer, while downstairs a mantel clock ticked in gleaming rooms filled with all sorts of people—men in tight-fitting black suits and white socks, and young women in short skirts and stylish haircuts, drinking tea and orange soda and talking about the weather as if the terms of it were a secret language for something much less ordinary.

In one week there'd been six funerals, and one day at tea, as Maureen O'Connor and I were arguing about who should have the last chocolate biscuit, the traffic on the Limerick road stopped suddenly and an unusual silence fell. Maureen went to the door, muttering, "God save us." I looked out the window in time to see a hearse followed on foot by a large dark-clothed group of mourners, there, then gone. Some people must leave a place, I mused, with fantasies of a glorious return. But sometimes there's nothing left to come back to.

———

Monaincha, the ruins of an ancient abbey and site of modern pilgrimages, sat in the middle of a boggy black field, which was once a lake, two Irish miles from town, its stone chancel, nave, and sacristy intact on a hillock. A few beech trees grew here, and it was quite peaceful, although they claimed that when the lake was drained it made a roaring sound and several skeletons emerged along the lake floor. At one time before leaving the country, emigrants would come out here and take leaves from the red-spotted creeper that once covered the walls; the spots were believed to symbolize the blood of Monaincha's priests and monks murdered by Cromwell's troops.

I went out there one day. The countryside was no longer spooking me as it did when I first arrived. Every few miles I saw these gothic-looking stone houses, owned by the area's more well-off; you heard stories about the people who lived in them, some involving incest, adultery, and other woes, which were, according to one publican, peculiar to the rich. The Slieve Bloom Mountains to the northeast rose out of a flat limestone plain. Cattle were raised in these mountains along with barley and oats, potatoes and root crops, and on the higher ground new forests with Sitka spruce and lodge-pole pine. But Roscrea's side of the mountains was more barren and covered with heath.

A children's writer lived out this way with her husband and a perky little dog, who was the subject of her books. Down the road from them, thrusting up from a jungle of weeds and vines, lay the remains of a distillery, which closed in the 1850s after its owners were exorbitantly fined for whiskey smuggling. A blue range of hills ran along the horizon. There were spruce groves and pastures, forest and cultivated bog.

At one point I came across a caravan of Travelers (Irish gypsies). The father was a tall man, with aquamarine eyes and a deep tan. As he hooked his horse up to a cart, his shoeless children, in clothes that may have once been colorful, surrounded him, giggling and looking at my face and clothes with frank, reckless gazes. My mother used to talk about the "tinkers" who lived near their farm when she was growing up in central Michigan. I wondered how ephemeral their sense of place must be.

Almost every inhabited part of the world has had its nomads. Irish itinerants were initially forced on the road by hardship and famine, picking up tinsmithing, chimney sweeping, basket making, horse dealing, and scavenging. The plastic that replaced the tin of the tinker's trade eventually thwarted some of their independence, and among Roscrea's older generation there was a small percentage of settled tinkers. Many modern Travelers, as they were called, depended on the dole, but it was still an archiveless, day-to-day existence; a catastrophe could be left behind as easily as a toothbrush; and home existed in the mind.

A teenage girl leaned from the Dutch door of the caravan trailer, smoking a cigarette and bouncing a baby against her hip.

"You're an American, are ye?" She had a broad flat face, eyes set far apart, and freckles scattered across her nose. She smiled. Her teeth were wide and unevenly spaced. "You have that kind of talk. Is that gold?" She nodded toward my pinky ring. "Would you give it to me, you would."

—⁓—

Father Doyle, who occasionally preached against emigration, invited me to tea at his house on convent hill. His study was crammed with piles of papers skewed off chairs and desk corners while other piles rose up from the floor like stalagmites. The shelves were filled with spy thrillers, a few political histories and nature magazines, and amid all this, a few pieces of African sculpture and a telescope. The kitchen was an immaculate showcase of modern convenience compared with most, with tiles and chrome where you'd normally see linoleum and plywood.

In his late thirties (I'd guess), Doyle had a puffy, docile face, brown eyes, and flat brown hair. He was popular with

parishioners although his sermons were difficult to understand because of the church's lousy sound system. I asked
someone about this—a housewife who wished to remain
anonymous on this "issue"—and she said, "That's how we
like our sermons. Mysterious."

We sat in the kitchen against the wall while he absently
swung the pinecones hanging down from a cuckoo clock,
his hand resting on top of his head.

"We're very much an alcohol society," he said, in a pon-
derous mood. "Especially underage, which will show itself in
the future. Schools don't give enough kids confidence in
themselves. An American sixteen-year-old is more confident
and articulate. There's no entertainment except for pubs, so
even if you don't want to drink you find yourself in an al-
coholic atmosphere. As for emigration, whether it be vol-
untary or involuntary, it's always sad to see them go. People
go because there's nothing here. There isn't work. What can
you do?"

He stood up and started to prepare "tea"—sausage, bacon, brown bread, fried tomatoes, potatoes, apple tarts, and
tea. As he talked, he gestured with a fork, his face growing
flushed over the heat of the stove.

"The major social problem has been this to-ing and fro-
ing. Whole families do it. They might have been on a
Mickey Mouse job with no future, but they wouldn't do the
same work here for social reasons. They see it as being beneath them, but in another country it's okay to take a
Mickey Mouse job."

We sat down at the table.

"There was one boy," he said between mouthfuls of food,
"who left because he wore a Mohican haircut and studded

leather jacket. He couldn't find work because of his appearance. You hear people saying all my friends are gone. It has a magnetic effect. Kids don't see it as a problem, because they've grown into it. Education was never seen as a priority in this community. Anyone with kids away at college, you know it was done at a real financial sacrifice. The emigrants I talk to find it lonely. They miss their home. The number of people dropping out of school has decreased because there's less employment opportunity. They stay on because there's nothing else to do."

As we talked I noticed there was some kind of ink reminder scribbled across the top of his hand near the thumb. I'd seen several Roscreans do this—write little notes to themselves on their hands—and it occurred to me that Doyle, who had the attention of packed masses all week, might have started this trend. Then, as if he'd read my mind, he said, "Everyone in Roscrea knows what is going on with everybody else."

OCTOBER

I appreciated our cold-water rooming house on the Crescent mostly for its desolate views. Out the kitchen window, for instance, there was a layer of brambles, stumps, and cement blocks in the backyard, and past this, the yellow stalks of a vacant field. The field was vital, always there, changing a little bit every day. The stalks bobbed in the talons of rooks and hooded crows. The seasons crept onto other seasons with leaves and seeds and ice. You'd expect to sometimes see a red umbrella or a broken kite, but you never did, and no one could remember what once stood there, although

surely something had. Some of the houses next to it had
been abandoned, and children avoided it; they crossed the
street. But this dissipated field with its stalks and black birds
reminded us every day that this house and the houses along
the Crescent—the boundary between order and instability—
hadn't been abandoned.

The Crescent itself lay on the fringe of Roscrea, just at
the bottom of Bunker Hill, which led straight into the heart
of town. In the other direction there was an area of abandoned houses and farther out a gray, grim structure to house
lower-income families. As a buffer, we had these empty
fields, a railroad track just over a knoll, the fire station, and
the library.

The owners of this house were now living in England.
After a succession of local women who had come and gone
like recurring winds, the house now had the symptoms of
irreversible domestic malaise—dented walls, shabby, cinder-
pocked carpet, warped doors, broken tiles, and wobbly door
handles and chairs—and I could feel that, at its very core,
the place had the soul of a halfway house. It had five bedrooms, a big kitchen with a range and a scrubbed pine table.
There was a living room with a fireplace, and a sitting room
you entered by French doors.

My room was isolated. It had a single bed with a striped
mattress, a flimsy armoire, a metal desk with no chair, and
always felt as chilly as a spring night.

Facing west out my window I could see the ivy-covered
wall of a doctor's office where red roses grew as wide as my
hand, and beyond that wall, the cinder-block yard, gabled
roof, and chimney pots of the house where my grandmother
Sarah lived for seventeen years. This proximity was a co-

incidence, ours being the only rooming house in town, but it made me feel I'd been heading in this direction my entire life, continually going east in order to face the west—the direction my family had always taken until I began to back-track.

What I did was chop my long hair short; it was the best way to keep it clean. I bought a hot-water bottle, and on very cold nights I wore my clothes and coat to bed and warmed my fingers over a candle to turn the pages of my book. I did a lot of my laundry by hand in water boiled on the gas stove, scrubbing the seams until blisters formed on my knuckles, then I hung it on the line in the alley although sometimes it ossified, underwear especially, and tumbled cheerfully toward the fire station in the breeze.

———

We had a gloomy sky all day but everyone seemed in high spirits. I raked the front lawn, then Anne and I drove up the street to buy a few bales of machine-pressed bricks.

On the way we laughed about the weekend crusades in Margaret's creaky bed.

"She's a humdinger, that Margaret," Anne said.

We also discussed housecleaning, which everyone had been having "bloody rows" over. Margaret always dumped her ashtray out her bedroom window and onto the neigh-bor's yard. Maisie, who had a colossal amount of hair on her head, washed it in the kitchen sink, and when Michael, Anne's fiancé, unplugged the drain for us he always pulled out something that looked like a horse's tail.

"They're a holy show, the lot of them," Anne said.

Later, as I was looking through some greeting cards in a

stationer's, a gray van equipped with loudspeakers creaked through town announcing the arrival of a presidential front-runner. It created a minor buzz in the streets and at dinnertime a moderate-sized crowd had gathered around his party's headquarters, a tiny building near Rosemary Square. We huddled in doorways and cars while a pluvial dusk fell fast on our backs, keeping conversations low.

When the candidate arrived more people emerged out of nowhere. He reminded me of a Florida retiree, with a long mineralized face, red-rimmed eyes, long teeth, and lots of oiled hair shaped into waves across his patrician head. The crowd edged him slowly into the back room of the headquarters and we all crammed in as tightly as possible with a nervous expectant energy.

His handlers were men with a privately educated look about them telling him where to stand and when to speak. On the table in front of him they propped three school-age kids as visual aids, sucking their thumbs in glazed bewilderment and muffling his speech, which was about and could not have been about anything but the importance of family. In 1937, Eamon de Valera, the Prime Minister, consulted the Code Sociale Esquisse d'une Catholique and various papal encyclicals while drafting the current Irish Constitution and extracted a few fundamentals. "The family is the natural primary and fundamental unit group of society," and "no law shall be enacted providing for the grant of dissolution of a marriage," and "mothers shall not be obliged by economic necessity to engage in labor to the neglect of their duties at home."

The candidate represented the conservative old guard, deeply rooted in the past. And because the past is something

Ireland would never run out of, they had controlled the political terrain since the 1930s and were in no danger of being ousted by new generations, because the new generations were on another continent and had no voting rights. Every seven years Ireland held the election of a ceremonial President, who is chosen for political reasons but constitutionally barred from expressing political views independent of Parliament or the Prime Minister. Regardless, a political fever had been rising since September, and Anne had been teaching me how to pronounce words like Taoiseach (Prime Minister), Bunreacht na hEraireann (the Constitution), or Aras un Uachtarain (the House of the President).

The candidate's most promising opponent was a young constitutional lawyer who opposed the ban on contraceptives, the illegality of divorce and homosexuality, and who had fought for women's rights and access to abortion information. She was a long shot in many respects but generally the feeling in our house was "Wouldn't it be something if she won?"

The candidate kept talking into the children's backs, unable to tamper with the image of which he was just a small part.

"It never changes," the young woman with raccoon eyes and military boots next to me whispered. "No matter how we vote, the government is always the same. Taxpayers paid for your man's kidney transplant. 'Twas in all the papers. Do you know where he had it done? That place with the Irish name, the Mayo Clinic, is it?"

Outside I asked a schoolboy clutching an overloaded book bag whom he'd vote for if he got the chance.

"Your man, of course," he said, then in reference to the

candidate's advanced age, added, "If only for the day off, miss. For his funeral."

—⁓—

Anne's brother Pat often dropped by. He spoke with a faint stammer, was a bit ungainly, and with his black hair and pale skin, left behind him a nocturnal afterburn. He was involved in church activities and collected psychotronic horror videos. Whenever I'd overheard him and Anne talking, the subject was money, him telling her how to save it. (Anne and Michael were saving to buy a house.) I'd never seen Pat smile or laugh; in fact, he tended to respond gravely and too literally to jokes and thought if he left Roscrea he'd lose his identity. It was apparent because of their different looks and dispositions he and Anne were adopted from different mothers. But as dissimilar as they were, Roscrea had a firm hold on both of them. They were orphaned here; this was where they were lost, so this was the only place where they could be found again.

Although it was afternoon Anne was still shuffling around in her nightgown. She'd just worked a night shift and after sleeping most of the day was now playing with my typewriter at the kitchen table.

"What's this yoke for?" she asked, pointing to the TAB key. I shooed her away because Pat needed me to type up his résumé. At the moment he was working at the Offray ribbon factory and at a gas station on weekends, and was now applying for a job at Antigen.

He handed me his curriculum vitae on a folded, lined piece of paper covered with a series of neat thorns and wobbly loops. I was used to the idea of one person's life generating a mountain of information; it could be that Ellis Island turned America into a bureaucratic nightmare with all those questions to be answered, but there didn't seem to be much paperwork in Roscrea; the bank teller still handwrote my balance into my bankbook for me.

Pat refused a cup of tea and stood in silence with this impenetrable air in his priestly black turtleneck. According to his résumé, he was twenty-four. But far from answering one question this prompted more. I rolled a piece of paper into the machine and asked him, offhandedly, if he knew anyone his age involved in the IRA.

"I'd shut my mouth about that if I were you," he said. I asked him why I should, but he just repeated himself a little more emphatically.

I typed.

He'd attended the Christian Brothers School. CBS, as it was known, was founded by Ignatius Rice to liberate Ireland from British rule under the maxim "Educate That You May Be Free." It meant then, as it did these days, higher education for the "common" people, but the Brothers were notorious for their violent methods. A few weeks earlier I'd walked through its empty halls. The door to the locker room was open and filled the main floor with the odors of urine and sweat. There was hushed recitation behind closed doors and generally a grim aura. I was hanging around the main office when the head Brother, a starchy, white-haired, slightly anemic man, swooped down on me in his razor-sharp black robe.

"Well, what do you want?" he demanded. I tried to explain but he cut me off and told me frankly that he thought my plans to write about emigration in modern Ireland were ridiculous. He did decide, however, to let me sit in on a chemistry class, where the teacher, a middle-aged woman, cowered under his gaze.

"Only photographs," he snarled, wagging a finger at me. "No questions, no talking to anyone!" Then he swooped back down the pissy hallway.

This was the place in which Pat spent seven years of— it would seem—bad luck.

"It was fierce," Pat said. "At CBS there was an emphasis on hurling." Hurling is a popular Irish sport, similar to lacrosse but played with broad-bladed bats. "I refused to play. I can't stand sports and politics; they sicken me. Drink, the same, it sickens me. But the Brothers are known for being academically better. A couple of the teachers there were downright evil. If someone was talking or being childish, they'd punch you really hard or hit you with a hurling stick."

He paused to push up his wire-frame glasses.

"I'd have done better if I'd played sports. It's not so good if you're shy and quiet. I'm religious, but I have to work on Sundays; anyway, our values seem to count for nothing nowadays." He continued after a jumbled pause. "There was and is a real push toward college. The competition is even fiercer today. It's one big rat race. The leaving cert determines your future, like, but third level leaves you overqualified for factory work, so you're neither here nor there. If you get a factory job, you're stuck for thirty, forty years . . . if it stays open."

Most of the employed young people in Roscrea were the lucky ones in a country where unemployment for those under twenty-five (half the population) had reached as high as 28 percent. Of the job applications that poured into Ireland,

30 percent came from emigrants—the unemployed in London and the illegal in the States. But, as far as I could tell, on a day-to-day level, the factories here left these young people feeling insecure and frustrated because of constant rumors of factory closings.

Pat still lived with his parents.

"I could save money if I wanted to," he said, a little guardedly. "The little bankbook is only a book, and £2,000 looks like £5,000. I had thought about emigration to the States. I'd have to start fresh there, no friends, no contacts, meeting the same wrong people, making the same mistakes, like being born all over. Going to the States, now, I'd see that as a failure while a fair few people would see that as a fresh start. They think it's the only way of getting on, but you can do that here, not as quickly, not as glamorously. Leaving Ireland is a big price to pay for success."

After a moment Anne burst back into the kitchen in her mother-hen mode, a grocery list in her hand.

"Need anything from the store, Joan? No? Then I'm off. Oh, St. Anthony, where are me keys?" She and Pat walked into the foyer, where they stood for a while whispering, I assumed, about money.

———

It was along a periphery road that I came across the Mahoneys' caravan—three campers and one barrel-top wagon. The grass around the campers was trampled, the road streaked with mud and washing debris; clothes hung in the bushes to dry, and there were rusting chairs, logs, and cigarette butts around a circle of burnt earth, the kind of wreckage that on close inspection marks a distinct territory.

Chris Kearnes told me, "Tinkers would live where you'd die," and despite several warnings from others that I would have the eyes stolen out of my head I went out there once or twice to talk to Sheila Mahoney and a few of her eighteen children. Breda, fifteen, who always lurked around as if invisible, usually met me halfway up the road, a tomboy with a blunt, freckled face and dull, curly hair. She wore a sweater stretched down over her knees and once told me about a weeping Madonna in the woods. "I'm not coddin' you, Joanie. Tears come out her eyes."

Sheila had invited me out—"Come tonight, you will. We'll have a chat and a singsong"—in her usual rapid-fire way, her voice scarred by cigarettes and alcohol. She was wearing baggy light-blue sweats and slippers. But while Sheila may have had an open friendly face, its essence was as impenetrable as a fern, her skin thermal, her hair an ashy blond. Her eyes were Appalachia blue, and a scar (the sickle shape of the Guinness bottle that caused it) cut through one eyebrow.

Sheila's camper was a bit more festive than the rest of the caravan. Family photos, brass urns, and vases sat along the windows. A car battery operated the television. There were two narrow benches covered with thin pieces of foam and one large convertible bed. The place smelled of sour milk, ash, and wet sugar, and a fire burned in a small unsteady-looking range, into which one of the youngest girls kept pushing her doll headfirst.

"Go away with that, Katie," Sheila hollered. She made us some weak tea and we sat on narrow benches. "In the summertime you can keep everything spotless. You can keep the childer [children] tidy and clean. In winter, you cannot."

Several children crowded in around us to get a look at me. There was no mistaking a Mahoney—they had wide leonine faces, thick eyelashes, pinprick cheekbones, and broad freckled noses. Sheila dressed them in charity clothes—stained patches, waists and hems fastened with safety pins, buttons gone or about to go, a multilayered, multifabric look—because no one gave money to a well-dressed itinerant. It was this slight deception that set the standard for all of Sheila's interactions with Settled, a proximity that in the five years they lived in Roscrea had slowly spiraled into adversity, creeping in like the weeds growing up around the wheels of these campers. It began when some of the children threw stones at a nun.

The family had been living in Carlow when at fifteen their oldest daughter came here to Roscrea to marry a cousin. Thinking there would be a wedding, Sheila packed the (then) thirteen children into two barrel-top wagons and traveled here in three days in the dead of winter, clothes frozen in the branches, burning trash to keep warm. She was nine months pregnant. When they arrived they learned that the wedding was postponed for two years because of a diocese ruling. So they stayed. The stones thrown at that nun drew the tenant world in rather than keeping it out. The nun helped organize a group to assist itinerants in the area. Shrewdly, they told Sheila the children wouldn't be baptized or confirmed unless she sent them to school, and because they were deemed too violent to mix with Settled children, a prefab classroom was built behind the convent.

For most of the children it was the first time they'd been in a building. They walked across long shiny floors, used

electric light, porcelain toilets, and some of them kept slipping out of the plastic contour chairs and onto the floor.

"The childer tormented me terrible," Sheila says of those
first years in Roscrea.

Despite herself, Sheila was drawn to the more stable life;
it was safer; tenant women lived longer and had fewer children, who themselves were less likely to die in fires or road
accidents. This yearning for roots seemed strongest in those
who didn't have it. She was thirty-nine. Since her hyster-
ectomy the year before she'd had more migraines and her
vision had dimmed.

At one point one of her older sons came into the
camper. He was haughty and tattooed, wearing brown jeans
and enormous skull rings on his fingers, called knuckle-
dusters, which were useful in fistfights. The small children
parted the way for him and he roughly but affectionately
grabbed them by the neck, then turned to me.

"Are you engaged?" he asked. "And your man, is he fat
or skinny? He'll do, eh?" The children giggled.

Sheila patted me on the knee. "He's only backguardin'
you." She turned and called to him, "Go on, now, get away
with that." She had an abrupt, scratchy laugh. In all the
commotion Katie successfully stuffed her blanket into the
fire.

One of the younger boys, William, wondered where I
was from, shyly twisting his fingers as he conceived of the
biggest, most distant place imaginable. "Dublin, England,"
he suggested, as if it were one place. I showed them an old
Life magazine I had in my bag. They studied it carefully,
awed by a picture of inner-city kids playing in the spray from
a fire hydrant.

"Are you from here?" William asked, amazed. "America," he said, giving it a Spanish twist.

"What kind of language do they talk over there?" Sheila asked. When I told her that New York was not a very safe place, she gaped at me. "Are you serious?"

"Sometimes we get a visitor at night," Sheila said, meaning police or social workers, which some itinerants call "child-snatchers."

The children turned on the TV, not to watch it but to sing along with the commercial jingles and the *Dallas* theme song. Sheila lit more candles and the faces around me suddenly seemed drawn in chalk. Outside, a herd of cattle passed so close on the road the camper rocked back and forth for a few minutes, which delighted the children. It was then I noticed some holes in the camper floor as cow shadows passed underneath; the holes seemed to have some practical purpose but I also wondered if they were there to reassure Sheila that the road was still right below her.

There have been groups of Irish itinerants who emigrated to the States decades ago, continuing their nomadic traditions along the Atlantic coast and to places like Georgia, Michigan, and Oklahoma. Traditions of any kind die hard enough, but for Travelers tradition was all the stability they had in the world, so it died, if at all, that much harder.

One of these traditions was their private language called gammon. I wasn't sure of the spelling, but "Staish a shade" meant something like "Be careful, here comes a cop."

The week before, Sheila had taken me to the cemetery to see the graves of some relatives. It was also traditional that an itinerant's grave be as lavish as possible, the most decorated in the yard. Some were decorated with whatever remained in their pockets when they died—tobacco, tin-smithing tools. "Traveling people spend a lot on their graves," she'd explained. "We go hungry for them."

There was another tradition too that, because it involved the death of a child, was that much more deeply rooted even as it uprooted them. It happened here a few years ago when the Mahoneys lived near the convent. A five-year-old Traveling neighbor of theirs had been hit and killed by a car. The family put all the girl's belongings—her school bag, clothes, toys—into the camper where she'd slept. At nightfall they poured petrol over everything, torched the camper and every reminder of the child; then they left the county before the next rain could wash away the scorched ground. Nearby, the Settled remember the pagan intensity of that funeral pyre: how the back windows of the camper blew out across the grass; how black smoke and flaming paper flew into the trees overhead; and how the metal frame sagged inward and folded into a charcoal mulch until nothing was left but the chassis, which lay there in the morning like the charred spine of some ursine monster. As social workers knew too well, this tradition alone made itinerants something of a housing risk.

Two itinerant women knocked on the camper door and Sheila stepped outside for a minute to talk to them. When she came back in, she said, "Their men are on the beer; they're looking for them. You get most them men would beat up their wives, but my Jimmy won't. He'd be off driving with the pony and cart and he'd go off for fire sticks and he'd help there to get out the childer in the morning. He's very good to get out the childer. He's the best in the world around kids for a Travelin' man, now, say you couldn't get better." One of the children whispered to Sheila and she nodded, then pulled something out of the pouch of her sweatshirt.

"Read it to me, you would."

It was a letter from Jimmy. He was in prison at the moment. It was gray and punctured where it'd been folded and refolded, and "censored" was stamped across the top. I read it out loud as Sheila and some of the older children excitedly whispered along with me the words they'd memorized. When Sheila showed me a blurry Instamatic of Jimmy, a combustible little man with red hair and an angular, impenetrable face, I wondered what could be more "settled" than prison?

———

My cousin Chris Kearnes reminded me a little of the Venus of Willendorf, wrapped in several sweaters and aprons, with laceless sneakers on her feet. The dark Mediterranean skin of her face was a mesa of wrinkles and scars. Her eyes were bright blue, and her arms as heavy and as strong as clubs. Her house smelled pleasantly of bread and clay; and, after sunset, the only light in the room came from turf embers and the TV at the end of the kitchen table. She sat all day in an armless chair by the fire, sometimes sleeping upright in it, never falling during these naps, she said, because her husband's ghost held her up.

The upstairs bedroom where her husband, Johnny, died had not been touched. His shoes were still beside the bed; strands of his hair still wound through the teeth of his comb. A small plaster Pietà sat on his nightstand, the blue paint of the Virgin Mary's robe having chipped into several varying shades. Beside the Pietà there was a bottle of laudanum expectorant years past its expiration date and a small plastic bottle of holy water long since dried up. He'd died five years earlier.

It all seemed to implicate the ruins this house was built on. Four years before Sarah emigrated, the house she was raised in was condemned by the government and torn down. I imagined this horrified her, having always been obsessed with appearances. It had been one of those quaint thatched cottages the tourist board is always pushing. The reality was that its thick walls constricted light and air and made them hotbeds for TB. Through subsidization new houses were built over these ruins, terrace-style with wide windows, hard floors, and chimney stoves. The front wall of Chris's house was painted a vanilla color and a gabled hood shielded the front door from rain. It had one main room with a small couch, a fire range, a gas stove, a sink, and a table that dominated the room in a space no larger than eight by ten feet. There was orange and green floor tile and blue windmills on the walls. Chris's bedroom was just off the foyer, and through a clapboard door and up some enclosed winding stairs there were two other small bedrooms, including the one where her husband had died.

Just to the right of the fireplace there was a pine credenza covered with a copious display of religious articles: dozens of Pope John Paul and Padre Pio buttons and medals, nightlights, eternal flames, and various portraits of Christ—with glowing heart, praying hands, upturned and downturned eyes, halos, dying, dead, and returned from the dead—popular saints, dozens of crucifixions, clock/calendars, seven varieties of the Virgin Mary, and in the foyer there was a shell-shaped holy water font (a symbol of St. Augustine's vision in which Christ told him he could sooner empty the ocean with a shell than understand the Trinity). I'd heard children call Chris the "holy woman," but she denied any special devotion; she went to church if the roads weren't slippery.

She and I had often had tea together. She was six when Sarah left and, like Sarah's father, her father had been a tailor. She remembered how he and her uncle Richard sat cross-legged to sew in the natural light of the shopwindow. But Chris was still reluctant to say anything about Mary O'Reilly.

"You'd draw the socks off a dead man, sister, with your questions," she told me. So we sat in silence for a moment. Water dripped in the sink; then she looked at me, laughed, and shook her head. "You're a queer girl."

At about five-fifteen Thomas showed up, as he did twice a day, to have tea with Chris, carelessly tossing holy water across his forehead as he entered.

"Don't believe a word she says, Joan."

"Thomas, will you sit and have your sup of tea?" she asked him.

"Not today, Mammy. Too much work ahead." He sat down and turned to me. "Do you know the tradition we have of getting rid of the old people in this country? We take a hatchet to them. Isn't that right, Mammy?"

"Oh, for fuck's sake, Thomas, don't tell her that."

"There's that word again. She's a great one for speaking the Irish, Joan."

Chris said nothing. Neither of them seemed distillable from the past and were known in town for their "old-fashioned" ways. Electricity was suspect. Chris thought the Apollo moon landing had permanently damaged the weather. And Thomas, in particular, was drawn to superstition and dour tales. One teatime he had a few more strange things to tell me, first about a Black Maria that had taken a delinquent girl away when he was young; "She was never heard of again," he said ominously.

"Another time, 'twas a very warm day in the month of June," he said. "We were coming from school and there was an ambulance going up a big steep hill, and the back of the ambulance opened. The man came out in the stretcher. He had a big shiny bald head. That's a true story. Another time, the picture hall burned. I remember the big hullabaloo in the streets. The sky was real red at night; we could see the reflection of the flames in the clouds. 'Twould murder you." He cut some bread, then stood up. "I'm going now, Mammy. Do you need anything?"

"No, Thomas, I'm all right."

"Then I'll go. Take care, Joan." He slapped more holy water across his shoulders. It beaded up on his wax coat and rolled off.

"God bless you, Thomas. Good luck, son," Chris called after him, as she did, twice a day, every day. "Thomas . . . Take care, Thomas, and good luck. God be with you." And then turning to me, she said, "The world would be lost if only for him."

———

It was toward the end of October that I felt this irresistible urge to get out of Roscrea. For one thing bad news had been trickling in from New York via the mail: a friend was getting a divorce; another's father had been murdered and the bizarre details of the crime were making national tabloids. If the world were simpler and people were guided only by the sun on the meridian, the motion of waves, and popular notions, migration could be consistently explained as the movement from shallow to deeper soil. But I could see it was more complicated than that. I'd been wondering whether Sarah had run away or gone looking for something, but now I recognized that the two struggles are sometimes one and the same.

So I went to northwestern Ireland, first to Sligo, the largest town in the area. It wasn't a big place, but it seemed at odds with itself, its streets straying when they should have connected, ending too soon, too suddenly, creating a wide perspectiveless landscape strung together by telephone poles and lime walls covered with spidery threats and boasts. White swans floated in the estuaries of the river Garovogue; a dense yellow light fluctuated in the clouds above them; and chimney smoke lashed against the ground. After a couple hours I knew that in Sligo Town if you were out for the getting, you'd be gotten. Your only protection against injury or intimidation might be a lit cigarette. I stopped at a grocery store and saw two men shoplifting a chemist's shop across the street. Up another street a shopkeeper scolded two little boys with bloody noses. Then, as I was crossing a wide avenue, a butch girl in leather snarled at me, "What are you looking at, bitch?"

The few people I spoke to only wanted me to explain myself, which I realized—holed up in my hotel room by nightfall—was both the benefit and the single misery of travel.

———

I left Sligo before dawn and alternately hitchhiked and biked north up the coast as far as Gweebarra Bay. A light rain murmured in the brown ferns, fuchsia, and holly; a purple range of mountains rose and fell to the northeast, and the wind grew icy, with fresh damp air and streams of smoke blowing across the valleys like erasure marks. The coastline was impossibly craggy, with tentacles of water spread deep into the land. Eventually I came to an enormous flour-white beach with dark sediment strips and razor grass whipping infinity signs into the sand. I met a Scottish minister here, who had the face of a Dutch burgher, stone pale, sand-colored hair, and wearing sand-colored sweater and sand-colored khakis like the cryptic coloration of an insect blending into the background.

"This is the most beautiful place on earth," he said. The tide was out and the beach looked as big as a desert. Just on the other side of the slat fences, however, stores and hotels stood deserted, with broken windows, boarded-up doors. Far from being an unreconciled part of the world, this area seemed quite resolved to itself, its deceiving look of virgin frontier, its campaign posters nailed to walls to be read by no one.

I turned south and rode from one village to the next seeing nothing but smoke and laundry—the rumor of civilization—until after dark when I returned to Donegal, where I had dinner at a cheap fish joint. Karen Carpenter tunes played overhead, and a blue fly zapper sizzled in one corner. The plastic glow of the place seemed inappropriate for Ireland, and I suspected the owner once lived in the States, and had been hopeful that certain features of suburban Yankee summers with their horseshoe pits and swimming pools would transfer to little Irish coastal towns known for dampness. At the next table some Americans—amateur musicians who worked for the railroad in Washington, D.C.—talked about dieting. It had been so long since I'd heard an American accent. Every word seemed too angular. "Big meal, very happy," one of them said, rubbing his stomach. They noisily invited me to their gig at a nearby pub. I accepted, and after a quick walk around town, went to the pub an hour or so before closing time. With its sea life, posters, lobster cages, sailor knots, and nautical maps, the place looked like a set in a children's theater. As I ordered a brandy at the bar, the man standing next to me rolling a cigarette announced that he was the son of an IRA hero, then glanced over to see if I was writing this down. I was not.

"That was the old IRA," he said, shrugging. "When they had some decency. You know the way, like. I'm Catholic, now, I was raised Catholic, but I can see the other side." He licked the edges of his rolling paper, pressed the cigarette into shape, then stuck it in the corner of his mouth. "Now, Jesus Christ, to me, was some kind of bloody genius all right, but I don't think he rose from the dead. Christ, no." He ceremoniously lit the cigarette with a match that flared dangerously toward his nose; he frowned not at the flame but at his next statement. "Catholicism has no propriety."

"Are you a German girl?" he asked. "They're all the time scribbling into little black books. Ireland is hot with Germans. They've come to buy it from under us."

He had once been a fisherman, he said, leaning over to

put his elbows on the bar. "But three of my best friends died at sea. Drowned, they did. Now, I've a theory about that. The minute you think you understand it, when you stop fearing the sea and think it won't get you, now, that's when it'll get you."

It was now after closing time. Throughout this discussion the Americans had been playing and by closing time had begun to pack up. They were so accomplished the publican kept handing them drinks and slapping them on the backs. Just as the Americans were about to leave, a toothless old man sat down at the upright piano, flexed his fingers, and began to play some dazzling Fats Waller. The Americans looked partly astounded, partly amused, their mouths dropped open, wondering if the joke was on them.

I turned back to the fisherman. "I'll tell you this," he was telling me in confidence. "I prefer the company of women. For one thing, they don't drown."

—◦◦◦—

Yeats's grave sat in the shadow of the Drumcliffe church's square tower that in the day's transient light had an almost unreal density; a stiff little Eden in the middle of nowhere, detached and wild with brambles, vines, and tree branches that had been shaped eastwardly by several decades of Atlantic winds.

The church interior was folksy, with cool dark shadows, aisles teeming with piles of flowers and lethargic flies, gold and blue enamel flowers painted on the organ and a half dozen red and golden apples arranged along a round altar like some spoiled child's private arbor. A woman wearing a thick blue coat and Cuban heels was good-naturedly hacking away at the stump of an enormous cabbage with a butcher knife.

"We had a harvest celebration last night," she said breathlessly. Her hawkish little face was covered in almost aboriginal streaks of rouge and blue eye shadow. "That's why all the flowers."

I asked her if I could make a grave rubbing of Yeats's grave; she paused, knife in the air, to look me up and down, but then she said yes, of course I could. After a moment she got on her bicycle, its basket bulging with roots and vegetables, and lurched head-on into a wind toward some distant rain streaking the sky.

I had brought sheets of tracing paper and a box of Crayolas to capture this memento mori, choosing a copper crayon. Because the stone was enormous and the day raw and cold, my fingers cramped up every minute or so.

When I finished, I walked back to the highway toward Sligo again, and eventually flagged down a rusty red truck driven by one of Ireland's rare imports, a Pakistani with teeth as dark as his hair. Through a hole in the floor of his cab I could see the road rushing below us.

"Mind you," he said. "Yeats was buried in a pauper's grave near Monaco and whoever lay buried there is some Gallic bastard with no shoes. So the theory goes." He smelled of cannabis. Before dropping me off at the bus station, he told me that he hoped my book would be banned. "Best thing for it."

Back at the bus station I asked the driver when we would leave. "When I've finished my tea, miss." This was as exact as it would get. I suddenly felt anxious to get back to Roscrea, even though I hadn't felt as if I'd really gotten away.

Before leaving for Sligo, rain and fog—"the lungs of the sea"—had descended and reduced Roscrea to a Morpheus ebb. Drinking had seemed more deliberate; dogs had stopped barking; and the mountain to the north had disappeared. It was as if the rain had gotten into my head and followed me, and by the time the bus pulled into Roscrea I'd convinced myself it was the one element that blinds our resolve. And still the darker clouds were shifting across an impenetrable bank of clouds, shielding us from the sun and the handful of airplane shadows that would have otherwise darkened Ireland that day.

———

I had tea with Chris to tell her about Sligo and Gweebarra Bay, which she found unimaginable. "You're great to do it, sister." She'd had a bad night, she said. "Dark dreams" all night.

"Let me tell you, now, if I dream of my mother or father, the light of heaven to them, the next day a knock will come to the door. I'll hear of someone dead, someone I knew. If you saw my dreams, sister, 'twould give you the fright."

Sometimes she'd reenact her most prodromal dream. "I was dreaming all night . . . there was something terrible wrong. I was dreaming all night of muddy waters. Deep, deep waters. The next day—I'm not having you on, darling—the next day I learned that Maggie, one of my sister's childer, who I raised my very self, had died. You'd want to be in a mental home if you saw my dreams."

When Thomas joined us we were still talking about them.

"I'd say she has second sight," Thomas agreed. He was

about to add something more when there was a knock at the door.

"Now, who's that?" Chris asked. "Thomas, go see, will you?"

Thomas opened the door and a squat little man in a sharkskin suit pushed his way into the foyer.

"Blessings on all in this house," he said, bowing to Chris and then to me.

There was a gold ring on his pinky finger, and he pulled an enormous wad of cash from his pocket, flipping it around for a moment, pointlessly, then shoving it back in his pocket.

"Well, what do you want?" Chris asked harshly.

The man held up his hand dramatically, then dashed back outside, returning with a rug sample which he stuck between his knees as he dug around in his pocket, finally producing a butane lighter. Without a word he held a corner of the rug against the flame.

Thomas's eyes widened and he turned to Chris. "It's fireproof, Mammy." With a twinkle in his eye, the man proceeded to tell Thomas that, in effect, if he didn't buy this carpet from him right now, well, it was the same as child neglect.

Chris stood up and started waving the man back out the door. "Fuck off and take that thing with you," she yelled. Thomas followed the man outside, where they talked for a while. Chris looked out the window, muttering. Finally Thomas came back in, convinced that after buying £100 worth of carpeting, he'd gotten one over on the salesman.

———

Halloween. In late October the sun rose halfway down the southeastern horizon toward the place where it would rise in the dead of winter. Fires had to be lit to ward off evil spirits, and itinerant children dressed in costumes knocked on doors, asking "penny for the Pooka." The Pooka was a misfit animal spirit who lived among old ruins and had, according to legend, grown "monstrous with much solitude."

In the packed-dirt courtyard of a housing estate several children had collected old furniture, garbage, and wood. The pile grew higher and higher all day as the wind howled; skirls of paper blew into the air and the sun gleamed off puddles as if imperiled. By late afternoon the pile grew more complicated—rug samples, aluminum cans, clothing—and by nightfall it had grown the size of a small grain silo. All this was soaked with lighter fluid and set on fire, then the children—all bright sweaters, red cheeks, and dirty knuckles—joined hands and circled around in a berserk game of ring-around-the-rosy. This game had its origins in the Middle Ages: the "ring" being the red rash of the plague, the "pocketful of posies" believed to keep sickness away, and the "ashes" those of the corpses burned in "bone fires," or bonfires, to prevent further scourge. Oblivious of this bleak history, the children danced and yelled and screamed savagely while throwing aerosol cans into the fire, which exploded and sent thumb-size pieces of cinders out into the dirt. Parents stood talking about the weather and the length of the day; someone told me that in November some men stop drinking for the entire month to show respect for the dead.

A little girl dressed as a tarantula came up to me. "You're

that American girl, are you?" There were gold hoops in her ears and a feral look in her eyes, and while we watched the fire she waved her many arms in the air.

"Do they have such lovely fires where you come from?" she asked. I told her no, but later it occurred to me that, being the descendants of those who built and survived them, we all come from such fires.

—⁓—

I ran into one of Sheila Mahoney's children, eight-year-old William. The Traveler boy was begging in front of the "Catholic" grocery store, but when he saw me he put his hands behind his back. I invited him to the tea shop above the grocery. Last year he'd been hit by a car and suffered a broken leg and torn ligaments, so he limped up the stairs. He ordered a rock bun and dropped seven lumps of sugar into his tea, half crouching on his chair as he studied the walls and the silver railings, counting chairs and tables. When he finished his bun he explained in detail how he would change this place; he had it all worked out. First he'd move the tables around so there'd be room for more chairs. Then more people would come in, you see, so he concluded that after a while you'd need more dish detergent for all the extra dishes you'd be cleaning. His eyes grew wide at the thought of this and he sat down to sip his tea for a while.

"Shall I write?" he asked. I gave him a pen and paper, which he labored over for several minutes, writing a letter to my mother in America. Then he drew some pictures. Watching him struggle over the paper made me think of how these buildings and tables and chairs that so intrigued him might one day betray him. They might weaken his ability to thrive on the road or off, blunting his "road reason," which was the ability to assess a person quickly, to barter horses, sell, and wheel and deal, and yet because he started school late in his life and had few role models he might never excel at academics—although there were Travelers with master's degrees—at least not enough to keep him off the dole or quite content to stand for hours on a factory floor. He chewed on a sugar cube as he wrote down all his brothers' and sisters' names. Then, after a second cup of tea, we went back downstairs. Outside, William headed toward another doorway, waving to me as he limped away, like the transparent boy in one of his drawings, not quite moored to his surroundings.

NOVEMBER

I first met Hugh Beck at the police barracks while chatting with the sergeant about crime in Roscrea. There'd been no murders, the sergeant had told me, and only a few serious crimes like assault, burglary, and vandalism. Dublin criminals were the biggest threat, those who'd widened their criminal circle, and who, like so many others, were just passing through. The sergeant had been shot two years ago during a robbery at my bank (which had been robbed so often it was nicknamed Billy's Take-Away), but still he felt safer without a gun.

Hugh, being the town's only plainclothes detective, did carry a gun, which he kept hidden under the down-filled parka he always wore. We met again for a pint one day as an early darkness rolled in off the hills. The town seemed strangely empty, and there had been a frost the night before, putting us on the edge of winter. The pub was cold and we shivered in our coats.

Hugh was tall but slightly hunched, with gray hair, a beard and mustache, arched nose, and blue eyes like crushed glass, all of which gave him the look and physical candor of Walt Whitman.

He told me about the man who shot his wife because she wouldn't make brown bread, which was the sort of anecdote every detective in the world could tell; there was a common language between those who go in to collect evidence after the dust and nitrocellulose have settled, but Hugh's stories still struck me as peculiarly Irish. As someone who'd never set foot off this island, he reminded me of an old Hindu taboo in which the faithful were not allowed to pass over salt water.

Hugh was born in a small cabin in County Wexford to a family of five children. His father, an insurance man and an amateur veterinarian, attended a separate church from his wife to avoid giving confession in front of her. His mother was active during the War of Independence, carrying dispatches and weapons, organizing safe houses, and acting as a decoy. She was also known for "making the best tea" in the area, which meant that she could read. Farmers brought their letters from America, Australia, and Africa for her to read by lamplight along with the daily paper, ads, and death notices. In exchange, the men told ghost stories, which Hugh listened to while looking at the stars through the open chimney.

Hugh wanted to be a fisherman, but his mother said it was too dangerous, so he drifted from job to job, trying farming, carpentry, lumberjacking, and sheepshearing.

He told me another work-related story: It happened somewhere east along the coast on a moonless night. He'd been called to the house of a fishmonger who lived with her two sons with no electricity. When Hugh arrived she and a son were sitting in front of the fire. Hugh chatted with them, gradually wondering why he'd been called. The fishmonger seemed unable to tell him, so as discreetly as he could, he looked around the place. Even when he discovered the fishmonger's other son, who'd hanged himself in the closet, the two sitting by the fire were unable to say anything about it to Hugh or to each other.

"The mother wore a long black shawl that pooled around her feet," Hugh added, hunched over the table with his fingers around his pint. The pub suddenly felt colder.

Hugh called himself a "peeler"—a disparaging term inspired by the unpopular, anti-Catholic Robert Peel, who established the Irish police force in 1814—and had the same vague mistrust and dreaminess as some Vietnam vets. When the troubles broke out in the 1960s, he'd been assigned temporarily to border patrol along a demolition belt in the North. But he didn't like to talk about it. "I got a little scared now and then."

Over the years he'd worked in various towns and counties and eventually rose through the ranks by specializing in technical backup, forensics, and ballistics. These days in Roscrea 50 percent of Hugh's job involved counseling family conflicts.

"Much of it is depressing and it's like you're playing God," he said, hunching still further over his pint and ashtray, sometimes rubbing his hands together against the cold with an anguished smile on his face. "Mind you, you meet them in the street the next day and they look away. My training was pretty slim. I don't think six months qualifies you to be turned loose on the public. I've spent years working the streets, days permeated with crime, subversives (IRA), as often as three times a year, debauchery, prostitution, and sudden death (suicide). It gets boring," he said, laughing. Hugh's laugh was not particularly contagious; you'd think he was ignoring a broken rib.

A few years before, girls under seventeen who became pregnant were treated as rape victims, so Hugh had to conduct "criminal" investigations, a series of questions about the "perpetrator" and the exact nature of the "crime." He remembered one such grueling interview at a home for unwed mothers. For the girl's sake as well as for himself, he tried to get through the questioning as quickly as possible, but he found it hard to concentrate because a nun was standing behind a screen throughout the interview.

"Her black shoes stuck out from behind the screen like two dead birds."

Another time he'd been sent to escort an old man to the mental hospital, which he'd done many times before. They'd talk and have some tea and then the two of them would go to the hospital. It'd become routine. But one time, the old man held a carving knife against Hugh's throat, and Hugh, who'd always wondered what the old man might be capable of, waited patiently under the knife, "tempting Providence." The old man finally relented and put the knife down. Explaining why he didn't disarm the old man, Hugh said, with a twisted smile, "I didn't want to hurt his feelings."

—ᴡᴡ—

Election day—Lizzie O'Connor picked me up after her shift at the nursing home. The daughter-in-law of Maureen, the cousin who'd found me a place to live, Lizzie was a boisterous, fleshy woman with bright blue eyes and an infectious, fun-loving personality. She had been promising me a home-cooked pheasant dinner for some time.

When we arrived at her small but rather modern-looking house on the edge of town, sunset filled the kitchen with a thin orange glow.

"Close all the windows. Make sure there's a good fire on." She hustled around the kitchen, chatting, becoming distracted and stopping now and then to ask, "Now, what was I doing?" She had five children. One boy had been born with spina bifida and was now in a wheelchair, but their shelves were decorated with his athletic trophies. The children drifted in and out of the kitchen. "Look at ya, just look at ya," Lizzie said to them, breathlessly, as if they were made of clay, taking on new and unexpected shapes every day.

"We're paid to have children, Joan, did you know that? The government gives us a monthly stipend per child. Not very much, but just the same, they give it to every family, no matter what their income. It's like a paycheck for housewives." She laughed at this. "You must think we're all mental."

Her oldest daughter dropped turf into the range, smiling at me as if I were going to whisk her away from all this. Out the back kitchen window I could see the garage full of turf and the hedges along a green pasture. Beyond these were two springer spaniels, excellent hunting dogs, judging from the number of taxidermic animals in the living room.

Lizzie prepared the pheasant, which her husband, Dennis, had caught. Pheasant was leaner than chicken, so it had to be aged—dangled from one leg until the meat had just begun to spoil. (With pheasant you didn't cook the flavor in, you cooked it out.) Brussels sprouts and potatoes boiled on the gas stove until the windows steamed, and Lizzie, who could make anything seem like an adventure, chatted excitedly about the possibility of seeing a popular talk show in Dublin.

At about six o'clock, Dennis, a stout man with thickish features and thin blond hair, arrived home from work at the telephone company; he was always friendly and funny, but at the same time he seemed reserved, a little mistrustful, as if he believed that my being here would disturb Roscrea's fragile ecology. He was probably right; when we sat down to the table, I asked him who he was voting for, reminding him that his own father planned to vote for Mary Robinson. He ignored the question; his candidate had just been implicated in a career-damaging scandal.

"You're opening a can of worms with that," Lizzie warned me, a mischievous look in her eyes. "I'm voting for Mary, you know yourself."

After dinner, Dennis, Lizzie, and I left the dishes for the kids and drove to the Boys' National School polling booths. On the way, Lizzie was barely able to curb her excitement and kept glancing back at me with huge eyes; Dennis drove in silence, his knuckles white on the steering wheel.

I waited outside surrounded by deep twilight. It took

about four minutes for them to vote and get back in the car. After that, in more silence, they dropped me off back at the house, where I ran into Anne at the door.

"I'm on my way to vote, Joan. Will you come along?" We walked through town toward the Protestant primary school. By now the streets were dark and there was a cold breeze that pushed our breath back into our mouths as we talked mostly about her adoption. Just that year she'd written to the nuns in charge of adoption records asking where she could find her birth mother. They'd told her that they had the information but they wouldn't give it to her. It was for her own good, they said, and legally she couldn't do anything about it. So Anne planned to ask them again and, if she had to, she'd beg them for her mother's identity.

Again, I waited in the night air while she voted. I thought of the home for unwed mothers. In the old days, mothers were referred to by numbers, not names; one woman in town was so distraught after giving up her baby she began to push a doll around in a pram; and, according to rumor, during World War II some unwed mothers could not get back into Ireland unless they put their children up for adoption. As I waited for Anne, I noticed that the school lit up in the darkness had a heartening effect, the light practically boiling out of the windows. The two seemed linked: Anne's search for her mother's identity; Irish women voting for Mary Robinson, both trying to find some meaning beyond papal encyclicals.

Later that night at the house everyone hung around to watch the news. Kate sat in the corner chair in her pajamas twisting a section of hair until it stuck out. "Joan, did you know that the scales of justice in Dublin were made uneven by a hard rain and they had to drill a hole in the one to even them up?"

Everyone screeched with laughter. Anne hopped around the kitchen slamming pans around; bookies had been laying huge odds in favor of Robinson. Now and then Anne came into the living room, where I lay on the couch, to nod at me, hands on hips, and say, "See now? Our little country's not so bad. Write that in your little notebook."

"You're lucky to be here for all this," Maisie said. She sat smoking a cigarette by the fire, her wet hair in a towel turban. "Really now. It's something."

Margaret came in from the kitchen furiously buttering a piece of bread and pacing. "Although I suppose it doesn't matter all that much. Not really now. But it's the idea of it, Joan. It's something different, like, you know the way."

———

I'd started to walk up the convent hill in a warm drizzling rain toward Templemore, but before I got very far I came across an enormous abandoned building set back from the road. It was not abandoned in the touristic sense—a charming ivied ruin—but looked more like something cannibalized. No effort had been made to board it up. This was the hospital Lizzie told me about that had closed about a year earlier. Now the closest hospital was twenty miles away in Nenagh, although Lizzie said there was talk of that closing too. " 'Twould be devastating," she'd said.

Ironically, the hospital itself had become an accident waiting to happen. I got in through a ground-floor window. Kids had sprayed graffiti across every wall, which gave the place the look of modern warfare. Old-fashioned graffiti. I was used to New York's graffiti, an amorphous, undecipherable language of its own. But on the walls of this hospital, there seemed to be no time for that kind of ingenuity. I walked through room after room of falling rain; it was the finality of the squalor that shocked me—the broken toilets, overturned medicine trays, aspirator bottles, rusted examination tables and gurneys, forceps, leaky sterilizers, and the shalelike layers and confetti colors of several different paint jobs falling across floorboards. Nothing had been salvaged. Yet out of that wreckage, raw persuasive assertions were being made. Mostly "Fuck off," but also simple testimonies about politics, ownership, society, existence, and love. Along one husk of a corridor I found "Caitlin was here" several times. Caitlin was probably somewhere else by now, in London or Cleveland, but her name was here and would stay here as long as the wreckage stood.

—⁓—

Even though the votes had been finalized and Mary Robinson was officially Ireland's President, Nuala, a young teacher at the Sacred Heart convent, didn't think this victory would have much effect on everyday reality. She was a bright, independent young woman with the kind of wiry hair and an old-fashioned toughness that inspired ballads. We met for a drink at a Rosemary Square pub, the only women in the place other than the woman serving drinks behind the bar, which was lined with a gloomy troupe of men. The bartender exchanged thumbs-up with Nuala.

After overcoming dyslexia (for which she'd been beaten every day with a tree switch in primary school), Nuala earned a three-year degree in biology, sociology, and theology from Maynooth Seminary and College, a small but diverse seminary.

"One of my lecturers said to us, 'You all get out. This is a seminary, not a whorehouse.' The place also shattered my nice little illusions. I went in believing in miracles, then found out some things in scripture were meant symbolically. I mean, in Ireland there is this veneration of Our Lady, the perfect woman, the virgin every man has to marry and the virgin every woman has to be. Basically the church is a great idea, but as an institution it needs a great clean-out. Psychiatrists or mental problems of any kind still carry a deep stigma. They'd rather see you take Valium than unload your problems."

Because she hadn't qualified for grants, her father, an accountant, paid her college fees and she worked in a creamery as a clerk and lab technician.

"I wouldn't get into college now. It's all gone crazy since I graduated; there are a lot of holes. Fees and costs have doubled and I'd be financially hammered. What you need to realize is that the Irish education system is the greatest maintainer of social status."

After getting her teaching diploma, she trained in inner-city Dublin, Ballymun, a bleak housing project on Dublin's North Side, where one of her students died from inhaling hair spray. Since then, most of her college friends had emigrated.

"They had to, not because they wanted to. There are very few jobs in education. My own parents would die if I'd emigrated. I've considered jobs in England, but I don't want to go. Emigration has always been an important problem for politicians not to solve. The country couldn't afford it. You can't create employment. Then you'd have to pay huge grants to companies and tax relief, and then you're left with empty factories . . . so they might as well pay the dole.

"In the classroom the Catholic ethos is high," she said, settling back into her chair. "I can talk about condoms, but I can't recommend them, and that's a mistake. I think it's almost irresponsible as educators not to teach the students everything about health." Before taking the teaching position, she'd signed a contract declaring that she'd protect the Catholic ethos. So now, if she discussed condoms with a student, she'd be fired. Not long ago Ireland's conservative forces had put out a pamphlet entitled "67 Reasons Why Condoms Spread AIDS," she told me grimly. "The government also always tries to make education look better than it is, but it's no longer relevant. Jane Austen is useless."

She planned to leave teaching and study massage therapy and reflexology. She leaned over the table to show me the soft part of my palm that, if pressed hard enough, would relieve back pain. When she picked up my hand, some of the men at the bar turned to stare at us, and a thought flashed through my head: It's November; they don't respect the dead.

———

The day began on the Roscrea train platform in an early-winter fog in which cattle trucks disappeared and the train station dissolved to a faint outline. Sheila Mahoney, the Traveler with eighteen children, and I were waiting for the train to Cork. She'd gone inside the station to change. When she reemerged in a pink acrylic dress and black pumps with glass beads across the toes, I realized you can change your name or your past but the profligate energy of the road resolves in the face. Everyone on the platform watched her as she tugged at the ankles of her hosiery and called to a porter on the far side of the tracks.

"Do you have a light, boss?"

He jumped down and crossed over, a spry little man with huge ears, and reached up toward Sheila with a lighter, appraising her with one eye. Out of her usual context—one camper, a dozen children—she was conspicuous, which might account for the lengths she went to in order to shield herself and her family from outsiders.

" 'Tis a queer fog," the porter said. He lit her cigarette.

" 'Tis."

Much to her credit, Sheila was as relaxed around gawking strangers as she was with her own children, largely immune to them, as if focused on nothing but the pounding of her own heart.

The train arrived late, and we boarded, sitting across from each other. The trip went quickly, if not a little perilously around bends. Everyone smoked. When the porter came around they signaled each other like delinquents and held the smoke in their cheeks or stuck their cigarettes out the window. At one point the sun broke through and cast a cemetery in a bluish light. Some blessed themselves. Sheila, who'd been buying us bottled pints of Guinness and had stuck a cigarette in the corner of her mouth, blessed herself automatically although she hadn't seen the cemetery herself; she was more interested in the horses in the fields. It was ten o'clock in the morning, but I drank the Guinness without protest. As a matter of fact, getting drunk seemed like an excellent idea; I thought it might put us on common ground, although we were traveling together with quite different intentions. I wanted to see the harbor Sarah left from; Sheila wanted to visit her husband in Spike Island prison. It was my idea to travel together, her idea to sneak me into the prison to meet Jimmy.

"You're all right, Joanie," Sheila said as we clinked our bottles together. "Me and Jimmy was never a day from one another until the day he got jail." We bought rounds and toasted each other and talked about horses, fog, and children. After a while we talked less and less and just looked out the same window.

We must have had three pints of Guinness each before we reached Cork, which seemed to have a rough edge or at least be the rough edge of the country (the way Marseilles and New Orleans are), a mixture of Georgian houses and aging mercantilism with a salty breeze rising from its parks, carved by random channels of water. It was an important brewing, distilling, and oil-refining capital, but for me "Cork" conjured images of anchor tattoos and ironmongering, and some of the old limestone architecture felt sulfuric as if *it* corroded the air and itself remained immune to the elements. I'd passed through here once before and had found an abandoned Protestant church covered in moss and condensation in the middle of a block of family businesses. Blasted from its roots and submerged, this sad, lightless place had reminded me of an antebellum plantation, except "Brits" and "Fuck the RUC" had been sprayed across its back gates. The Guinness may have been adding weight to my perceptions that day or maybe it was just that since morning our mood had changed as the world shrank in our minds down to a space no larger than the size of a prison cell.

In the train station it was understood that we'd have another pint, especially now that we were so near to Spike Island prison. I bought some ham and butter sandwiches, which we ate silently, watching the workday pandemonium around us; then we hailed a cab.

" 'Tis a funny place for a prison, isn't it, boss?" Sheila asked the cabby. His red neck lay in folds and he leaned so far over against the window he might have been asleep. But his eyes watched Sheila in the mirror, as if he recognized her "race."

"Aye," he grumbled.

By now the morning fog had lifted, but the sky remained dismal, clouds lying in low, humid layers across the horizon as the cab circled down into the little harbor at the mouth of the river Lee, to the beautiful but ill-fated Cobh, the *Titanic*'s last port of call and the leaving point of countless emigrants.

The cab dropped us off in front of a sawdusty little pub near the docks. We had about a half hour before the prison tender crossed to Spike Island. The pub, like the streets, was empty; it smelled of hot paraffin, but Sheila seemed to know the bartender, a hard-edged woman with short black hair and a high shiny forehead. This was Sheila's most disarming quality: acting as if she knew everyone until they began to believe it themselves. They talked about hairdos.

"We'll tell them you're my daughter, won't we," Sheila said, turning to hand me a fresh pint of Guinness. We absently clinked our bottles together. As we walked down to the pier, Sheila brushed my hair over my face in an effort to hide what wasn't there. There were eight or nine others boarding the tender. The guard, an early-retirement candidate, watched everyone—his eyes flickering uncritically at me and my unreadable registry signature. After a while, with water lashing dark contours against the bleached pilings, the boat chuffed across the deep-water harbor as a mist began to fall in all directions and the shore shrank away the way it shrank away for Sarah in 1912—the year Bram Stoker died, the year cosmic rays were discovered.

I felt a pang of dread about Roscrea and my relatives. They were telling me things about Sarah I already knew. For instance, she'd been seasick during the first few days of her voyage until a priest offered a remedy—probably theophylline, a substance derived from tea leaves. Once recovered, she danced across the Atlantic, but I needed to know more than this.

I looked out toward open water. Different migrating birds favor different navigational prompts, like infrasound, shoals, or stars. Back then the Irish favored far less reliable sources, like postcards and the propaganda of ship companies. Their first sight of America was probably Fire Island, an ever-narrowing barrier along the coast, so named because of land pirates who lit fires to lure ships off course.

After about ten minutes or so our prison tender landed. Everyone disembarked in silence and followed the guard up a road that seemed to go nowhere past one abandoned house after another, our arms folded against a chill in the air. By now the Guinness felt like tar in my head; Sheila and I were both sobering up with every jarring step, as the road crumbled away on both sides. It looked as though, in another year or so, it might vanish altogether.

After several minutes of walking we came to a cement-block barricade built into a grassy hill, where the road ended at two immense Alice in Wonderland doors, which seemed an appropriate entrance to a prison that wasn't visible until you were inside it. It was as if somewhere between their design and their actual construction, the place these doors had been built for existed only in someone's sick judicial imagination. Two guards whispered into each other's ears for a moment, then swung the doors open onto a dark passage and to a courtyard of green weeds sprouting up through an upheaval of cement. The building on the far side of this looked like the skeleton of some defunct consulate, but we only glimpsed this before being herded into a barrel-vaulted room of painted brick where we sat along benches built into the wall. Sheila was looking pallid and more single-minded than ever.

"Nights is long," she said to the woman sitting next to her.

" 'Deed they are."

For months, prison and Jimmy had been like two blind men about to collide. His pony had been stolen. (More than anything, the quality of a Traveling man's transportation reflected his status.) But the incident only fueled rumors that he'd stolen the pony in the first place, and the rumors grew until Jimmy was no longer asked to drink around the campfire at wedding celebrations. He became despondent and drank more. According to a couple of people involved with the case, one night he smashed a garda's window and never paid the fine. Some weeks later he lashed a Settled man with a horse whip during a minor traffic dispute.

"He give him a few welts with a little light stick," Sheila

tried to explain to me in the way she had of making plain fact seem not only refutable but foolish. "Just caught him there across the face. See, he didn't know what he was doing. Sure, he hit me a slap too, but he didn't know he was doing it." One day Jimmy assaulted a cop and that was that. "When they took him away," she said, "the roars of me."

Jimmy told the judge he'd been "tormented." Now, even in prison, he was transient. First, they sent him to a Limerick prison, but after too many brawls, they transferred him to Mountjoy in the North, then to Cork, then to this prison you couldn't see until you were inside it, where he swapped clothes and boots and did whatever else he could for the illusion of change.

The minutes dragged by. Finally we were escorted into the adjoining visiting room, which was identical to the waiting room but with a long table down the center, a grimy glass partition bisecting it. Two guards sat at either end of this on tall stools, gazing at nothing in particular. The prisoners filed in wearing bright green sweaters with yellow insignia and blue jeans fresh off the sewing machine.

Jimmy sat down behind the partition's fog of fingerprints. His skin was so raw he looked as if he'd been ice fishing for the past few months and his nose was bent at a distressingly abstract angle. He nodded shyly at me. His lips were mottled and he folded his hands together gently, as if they were liable to break. He was polite, but he also had this surprising peacefulness and was not at all the tightly wound spring that I'd expected. In fact, he seemed to have an almost Zen-like tranquillity. Sheila and he barely glanced at one another. She was all business. She was going to have a chat with the "governor" about getting him out soon.

"A few of the childer need new shoes," she informed him, then added as if there was a connection, "Paddy has been stabbed." Jimmy nodded; he'd heard. Now and then he slipped into gammon, but it didn't matter either way, because his complex accent was impossible for me to understand.

The visit didn't last long and soon the whole process reversed itself. The prisoners filed out. We filed back out into the waiting room, out the Alice in Wonderland doors, and back down the vanishing road, onto the boat, and across the bay. Everyone was silent but the mood felt a bit brighter. The shore grew in front of us across the deep water, colorful town houses, bright gables, and the open windows of the houses built against the hills. But I noticed that far from invoking beach balls and tropical drinks by the pool, the palm trees along Ireland's coastal waters felt slightly corruptive. This was true especially under a late-afternoon sky when the crowns of these trees, called cordyline palms (yields of drift seed cast into some North Atlantic gyre by a Caribbean hurricane), turned a deep sour green.

Sheila spoke once as we approached land. "Jimmy and me used to be everywhere together."

DECEMBER

The west side of the sky was still yellowish gray when I arrived at the Kellys'. Bridie Kelly led me down an unlit hall past an unlit sitting room and into the extended kitchen, which consisted of a narrow cooking area, a dining table, and, perpendicular to the kitchen, the main room with a turf range, chairs, and a couch directed toward the TV, which was at full volume.

The Kellys had just returned from Connecticut, where they'd lived on and off for years. They both came of age during the "hippie days" and now had four children. Bridie was a petite, nervous woman, likable but timid with a distressed face. Dick had a heavy, tanned face with a bulbous nose and large bloodshot eyes. His brown hair was thick and matted, and he was built like a bull. When I came in he stayed on the couch, feet on the range, staring at the TV, indifferent, it seemed, to everything around him, smoking one cigarette after another. They'd been home from America now for two weeks, and they didn't seem quite ready for things to retract around them. It was a full ten minutes before Dick even glanced at me. Bridie perched in a corner chair scrunched behind the range. I sat at the other end of the couch, keeping my coat on and yelling over the noise of the TV. They yelled back.

Historically, global migrant patterns were shaped by the weather, disease, the pursuit of food. In Connecticut, where Dick had been a construction worker, the pursuit had become one of water beds and Jeep Cherokees. "We had a telephone there too," Bridie said, looking at Dick first to make sure she wasn't about to interrupt him. "And clothes were cheaper."

"I wouldn't knock America," Dick said, his accent flattened, as if ironed out by America's unremittent industrial forces. "It's good. You can be broke today and you can go the next day and get work. It also made the kids more mature and confident. They're open-minded now and will discuss anything. It's a healthier atmosphere out there. In America everybody's equal." He spoke in phrases interrupted by pauses in which his attention fell on the TV.

"Nobody is watching to see what you're doing. . . . There can be a lot of bitterness here over religion. . . . Here you're not meant to get ahead. I would recommend going there to any single person. If you've got a family, forget it."

At that point one of the kids—a gangly youth—walked through without speaking or looking at us. When he disappeared back into the dark hall I suddenly felt these dark rooms were screens against something, especially when Dick referred to America as "out there," a force pushing down on Ireland, a force against those who returned and found their lives leveled by the welfare system. It was said that the unemployed in Ireland were less likely to attend church; they socialized less and had unlisted phone numbers. But it was also easier to be poor in Europe than it was in America; there was less stigma; they were less segregated and their streets and schools were safer.

"Coming back from America you have to adjust," Dick continued. "You have to play down America. You talk to your old friends as the person that they once knew, not who you really are. It's a little bit stifling, but you can't come back bragging; you hold back. Nothing has changed here. This is a friendly town. You're one of the people."

"They're really down-to-earth," Bridie piped in before retreating deeper into her chair. Now and then while Dick talked she'd gotten up to go to the kitchen to move things around, but returned to her chair as if overwhelmed, stepping over Dick's legs, then sitting and resuming her expression of dedicated interest in the conversation.

"It doesn't pay to work." Dick talked on, pausing now and then. "But I don't worry. I do what everyone else does. I go down and sign for the dole. I left Roscrea in the first place because I felt they were busting my chops. You've got people emigrating who've never been a mile away from cow shit. They go to another country and they're lost. You see, the government doesn't give a damn about emigrants because they're keeping down the unemployed."

He moved his legs one over the other on the range. "Why should I work?"

After a while Dick lost interest in the TV and started to look my way as he talked and even got up and cracked open the tab of a bottle of whiskey and poured us a drink.

When his father died, he left technical school and worked in a grocery shop, then trained as a carpenter for three years until he was nineteen, when he emigrated to Connecticut. He had been back and forth between America and Ireland for the past twenty years. During one of his return trips, he met Bridie at a dance. "She got on my nerves," he said matter-of-factly, then chuckled and coughed. She smiled and added, "We've been married for twenty-three years." The family had been back and forth about five times. He had one sibling in Roscrea, one in England, one in Australia, and one in America.

"Four years ago we lived on eleven pounds a week," Dick said. "Don't ask me how we managed. I used to be self-employed."

After a minute Dick clapped his boots together. "I got itchy feet. There was plenty of work in America at first. They love the Irish. But we had to leave because there was no work. The economy on the East Coast is bad."

We all sat without speaking for a while; then Dick jumped up to show me a wooden harp made for him by IRA friends serving time. He beamed over it, pointing out signatures on the base.

He got involved in the "subversive activities" when he was twenty-one. As he poured another drink, he said, "I don't care who knows it," relaying stories that sounded as if they'd been well worked over in some Connecticut bar.

He also used this house to hide prison escapees, he claimed, and subsequently, the cops would raid every few months to search the place.

"The general cop is okay, though. A lot of them are sympathetic."

"They were nice," Bridie chimed in confidently.

"I believe if England would get out of the North we'd have a beautiful little country. People in the North are not English. They're Unionists. There are no Unionists in England."

It was when I noticed I'd been sitting on toys and magazines for the last forty-five minutes that I realized how really suburban these two were. There was an unusual sprawl in this room, completely American and out of place on this street where all the houses were pin neat, newspapers stashed under cushions. But Dick and the family had to keep America to themselves; they had to turn back into something they weren't anymore. This casual housekeeping—which also seemed to have some hint of fear about it, as if putting the cereal boxes away and drying the dishes might suggest too strong a commitment.

Dick sipped his whiskey, stared at the TV, and with his

feet back up on the range said, "It's hard to adjust to the ashes."

———

That winter seemed to have no governing angel. Ships were lost off the coast, and when I walked out the few miles to visit Father Tierney at the monastery, the snow had once again reached blizzard conditions with gale-force winds. Tierney seemed to be uniformly admired in town. Everyone mentioned his name, atheists included, and I wanted to meet Roscrea's idea of a hero.

"From the spelling of the name I thought you might be some French broad," Tierney said when we met. I was pulling chunks of snow out of my scarf onto the polished floor of the monastery guesthouse, which looked like a big, respectable hotel a few years past its prime. He led me somewhere below all this to a little room off an unlit undercroft where a small window toward the ceiling was filling with snow as if to seal the room up. The carpet here was thin but unworn. Plastic orange coals covered the front of the electric heater, and generally the room had a Vatican II atmosphere—unctuously mod—the contrived homeyness of a renovated basement.

"Not many people come down here and when they do they get lost." Tierney had a voice that was deep and a little theatrical. He still had the burr in his speech left over from a youth spent in the Rathgar section of Dublin, where his father, who worked in a grocery store, loved books and the theater, and welcomed Balzac and Shakespeare as much as he welcomed priests and nuns into the house.

Tierney sat flat-footed, arranging his robe around him. He was stout and robust-looking, probably in his mid-sixties. He had a round, florid face and snowy white hair; his beard and mustache, he said, changed length and shape with the seasons. He had the air of a busy executive—one knee bouncing up and down—who in some other life would have owned an island and ordered crates of Iranian caviar. He called himself a "control freak," but in reality his entire life had been free of capital gains and insurance coverage. He didn't have a bank account, a credit card, or a dime to his name, although the agriculture and boys' school connected to the monastery were said to be lucrative concerns. His day followed a simple order based on one complicated idea, and Roscrea and its people reached him mostly through whispers. But you couldn't say that his life had been a stark and uncomplicated one; in fact, it seemed that these days Father Tierney would rather talk about Tennessee Williams than God.

"Williams succeeded in putting that stream of cruelty running through all of us on the stage with terrific starkness."

That was how the conversation went all afternoon, taking unexpected turns. I was trying to figure out how we began talking about American southern playwrights when he stood up.

"If you wouldn't mind waiting for a moment," he said, swooping out the door, leaving a current of cool air circulating through the room for minutes afterward. I waited. The heater made the room smell like a rock quarry and the snow continued to fall. Far away the church bell struck the hour or maybe it was from somewhere above, a chime inside a guest room.

After ten or fifteen minutes he returned carrying an enormous tea tray full of chocolate biscuits and soda bread and set it down on the conference table at the back of the room. "Now, where were we?"

He came here when he was eighteen. At that time he slept on a straw mattress in an open dorm along with about a hundred other monks, with only wooden partitions between each. He rose at two in the morning and worked in the fields, doing everything by hand. Fasting and malnutrition marked his vegetarian diet, with no fish or eggs and, at Lent, no butter. He ate soups, potatoes, fruit, milk pudding, and, on feast days, cheap wine. Mild illnesses lingered or intensified. Ulcers were common and healed slowly if at all, and food became a childish obsession. At eighteen, he had effectively cut himself off from everything that was familiar to him, and it was ten years before he saw anything outside its gates again. Conditions had improved a little in those years. He now had his own room, his own computer.

He poured us some tea.

"You come into a monastery to get away from people, but then you realize that God is with the people. A lot of people with problems come here to the monastery. Family and marriage problems. Children. Sometimes depression. Neurotic problems, sometimes problems about their faith. I remember a line from Edna O'Brien's The Country Girls. 'I'm in trouble. Jesus Mary there's only one kind of trouble.' "

During his two-year novitiate, he said, he experienced the loneliness and depression emigrants would feel, although

he was locked away inside the very country they'd left behind.

Helping myself to the cookies, I noticed Tierney ate
none, but drank his tea in one gulp.

There was a timid knock at the door. "What is it?" Tierney yelled. There was no answer for several seconds, then
another knock like someone testing a secret code. Tierney
charged over and opened it.

"What is it?" A monk stood in the shadows of the hallway: I could only see his fingers sticking out into the light
like withered orchids. They whispered for a moment. Tierney growled, nodding impatiently, then disappeared for a
moment. When he returned after a few minutes he said, "I'm
impatient. I have this desire to dominate others, especially
those I consider stupid." He sat down and brooded for a
moment. "I identify with the ambition and venality of Mac-
beth."

By then the window near the ceiling had grown silent
and gray with snow cover. We talked about how emigration
often brought to question the viability of a place, and how,
combined with sin-oriented Catholicism, it had left the Irish
with a poor self-image.

"We should never have moved from Israel," he concluded.

When he was thirty-five, he was sent to Rome to study
theology at a Dominican university, where he eventually
received his doctorate. By then he was fluent not only in
Latin and Irish but in French and Italian as well. Before
returning to Ireland, Tierney traveled to Israel. His "cru-
sade" began on a quiet morning in Venice. In Petra he slept
in a police cell because he couldn't afford a taxi back to

town. One night he slept in a cave. He spent a week in Cyprus and hitched a ride on a motorcycle to Syria, where three continents merge. After twenty-one days of traveling, he reached Jerusalem, a city destroyed, rebuilt, destroyed again, divided, and now dependent not only on the fervor of three religions but also on diamonds, plastics, and shoes. I thought for a moment about this almost animal instinct we have to return to our remotest origins.

When he returned to Roscrea he worked eight years in the infirmary, administering extreme unction, enduring this until he grew too depressed and applied for leave to America.

"Nobody in Roscrea thought I'd ever come back. But I knew I would."

I kept wondering what had initially motivated Tierney to come to this monastery. His whole being seemed opposed to the quiet confined life. Not long before he entered Mount St. Joseph's, World War II was blocking the supply of tea, bread, butter and sugar, fuel, the kind of shortages that people tend to recall fondly. The Irish called World War II the "emergency"; but in Dublin stray dogfights roared over head, so close that Tierney could make out the pavonian circles on each wing and see the men inside; air raid precaution officials came around to fit gas masks onto the children. One night in May 1941, German planes mistook the lights of Dublin for Liverpool and dropped bombs, killing twenty-eight people. In a place like Ireland in 1944, joining a monastery was like joining the Marines.

In 1977 he worked in various parishes, mostly in California, for about a year.

"America is truly the land of freedom. Anything goes. If

you want to run pornographic films and the guy on the corner is running a church, they are both protected by the law." He found American churchgoers more open, more honest, and more likely to attend mass simply because they wanted to and not because it was expected of them.

"Why did I come back? I feel that if I left I would be leaving part of myself."

When he said this I realized that he was perhaps a "hero" in Roscrea because he was *here*.

It was well past dark, and we walked along the narrow undercroft through cold drafts in near-darkness in search of transportation.

"This is against the rules," he said proudly.

After a moment we bumped into a frail young monk with a long, prematurely gray beard.

"You know all the shortcuts, Father Tierney," he said, and then turned to give me a searching look. "I've walked miles in this place and still can't find my way."

Irritated, Tierney gruffly told him, "Go back the way you came." We kept walking until the undercroft opened up to the stables and garden of the monastery. The blizzard had subsided, but it was still snowing. Inside a cellar garage, we found a rusty little Vauxhall with loose doors, then drove out through the stable's courtyard and past the sentry post to the main road at a great speed; the mill whipped by, a dim geometric shape in the snowy headlights. Black ice appeared like road bumps through the drifting snow, but we reached the Crescent in minutes.

To Tierney, Roscrea was like any other Irish country town.

"Country people are different from Dubliners. They're

more suspicious, and it's difficult to be accepted. Even people who've been living in the town for years feel this. They are suspicious of Dubliners, those smart alecks from the big city; it's a slightly patronizing attitude, you know yourself." He hesitated, then said, "Joan, I'll think you're a dreadful little bitch if I don't like what you write about me."

I considered this for a moment, then asked, "Didn't you ever take the vow of silence?"

"No, I never did."

———

I ran into Detective Beck one day and we went to Christy Mahar's pub next to the castle, his usual hangout. Christy's was one of Roscrea's first renovated pubs, so rather than the lush velvet, oak, and brass atmosphere of the more recently renovated pubs, it had banquettes, wood paneling, 1960s light fixtures, and a mod Italian spy thriller atmosphere, which was probably unintended. And if Christy had his teeth in, it was a good night.

We sat at the bar, and Hugh waved a finger at Christy, who bounced nimbly behind the bar, a pink bald man with long thin legs that he would swing over his head to touch the upper beam of the doorframe for demonstration purposes. But only if he felt like it, only on teeth days.

Christy once said to me, "It's too bad about the American South."

"What do you mean?"

"That they didn't win the Civil War." I wasn't sure if he was pulling my leg or if his friend from South Carolina or Georgia or wherever had really gotten to him.

Hugh got nostalgic in this place. In the old days he and

his best friend Eddie came here. There was a plaque in honor of Eddie on the wall, with a poem he'd written. Ed had been a chemist at the meat factory, but he'd been known locally for his poetry and mordant wit. As if to make one last observation about what had become for him the unbearable conditions of Ireland, Eddie killed himself by jumping into a vat of cow offal at the meat factory.

"Suicides go unnoticed in Ireland," Hugh said, staring straight ahead for several moments before leaning toward me to tell me about a young boy who had accidentally hanged himself in a barn. What he'd never told anyone was that he'd discovered behind the barn a small grave the boy must have dug for himself earlier that day.

"I've never told anyone this story before . . ."

The death was ruled an accident. There was no real proof that it wasn't, Hugh reasoned, and besides, officially there were no suicides in Ireland. A suicide victim couldn't be buried in hallowed ground, so doctors generally made out two death certificates, one declaring the death accidental (with the assumption that the victim remorsed at the last minute but was unable to reverse his actions) and a second declaring it a suicide, which was kept in a confidential file. Ireland had the fastest-growing rate of suicide in Europe, with an enormous increase in the past twenty years among people aged twenty-five to twenty-nine.

Hugh and Kathleen lived in a modern stone house on the edge of the Christian Brothers' playing field. I'd been there one day, sitting at the kitchen table and talking with Kathleen for hours. She was trim, lively, enthusiastic, and adventurous—and had just returned from Iceland. She was born an only child in the southern part of Tipperary, studied nursing in England, and was now practicing podiatry and teaching yoga.

Their tomcat jumped in my lap and a little tan dog kept circling around us.

"Some people inherit money. We inherited a dog," Kathleen said, setting down a pot of tea and brown bread. She told me the saga of her grandparents. A marriage had been arranged for her grandmother to a man she hardly knew. Everyone tried to convince her that she might grow to love this man but she refused, even when they increased the dowry. One night her grandmother stole the dowry that had been kept in a locked chest and eloped to America with the man she loved. They went to Boston, married, then returned home after two years.

"She said she didn't like the heat," Kathleen said, "but I'd say she was dead lonesome. My grandmother and mother were great to write to relatives in America. This job passed on to me. I remember this one day, it was awful, the children were in nappies and between one thing or another I was exhausted and all I could think was: On top of everything else today, I have to write to America!" She groaned dramatically and laughed. She and Hugh met when they were both engaged to other people. She remembered sitting in a dark theater holding hands with both of them. "If we'd left Ireland we would have missed out on all the traditions."

They were both passionate conservationists. They hiked in the bogs and mountains and had a place on the southwestern coast with a sixteen-foot fishing boat.

At one point, we were looking through some cookbooks when I noticed some poetry scribbled over the pages. It was Hugh's. He scrawled poems on the nearest piece of paper whenever they popped into his head. He'd had some poetry published locally, but despite this, despite the three children they'd raised here, and despite the twenty-six years they'd lived in Roscrea, they were still considered "blow-ins."

CHRISTMAS WEEK

Some days a warm rain fell. Other days the rain froze everything into one silver sheet, and then it felt as if dusk would arrive just after lunch, the sun barely visible behind cold, dark chimneys. In fact, it had been a bad winter. Pleurisy had kept me in bed, and we continually ran out of turf. I spent evenings in front of the fireplace writing letters after everyone had gone to bed. In the day I left the radio on for talk shows, news, and the Angelus: this was the ringing of a slow, heavy bell at morning, noon, and night, to commemorate the archangel Gabriel's annunciation to Mary. Three times a day it filled the house with its slow, focused tones as austere as Irish Catholicism itself.

The Exorcist III was playing at the movie theater, an irreverence that might have amused James Joyce, who opened Ireland's first cinema in the winter of 1909. I took walks around the edge of Roscrea, occasionally followed partway by a three-legged dog. I'd been told that at Christmas returning emigrants were everywhere and seemed to double the population of Roscrea, but that year, for reasons unknown, Roscrea felt empty—a migrant's destination—with everyone staying inside, the pubs keeping unpredictable hours.

One night, however, there was a singing competition at a pub. It was well under way when I arrived. People stood on stools or sat on headrests, clapping and cheering for each singer—the worse the singing, the louder the cheering. Most of the music was American country and western. I ordered a pint of Guinness, although the drink of choice that night seemed to be Budweiser. My housemate Margaret called me over to her table. " 'Tis great gas," she shouted. "Sit, Joan, down by me." The girls linked arms and started to sway while wailing, ". . . bye, bye, Miss American Pie . . ." The pub had black mahogany tables and stucco walls, purple cushioned seats. Women wore jeans, leather coats, and high heels. There were a few older women in the crowd, who were easy to spot because they kept their coats on all night. When they were our age they hadn't been allowed in the pubs, and the coats suggested they hadn't quite adapted to the idea. In the old days there had been something called a pub/grocery and the women could stand in the grocery while the men in the pub handed drinks over to them. There was an orange, vaguely hellish glow across everything, the source of which I couldn't place. Margaret grabbed my arm and pulled me close. "We need a Yank's advice."

"Joan, will you teach us some obscene American sign language, you know the way like. What you use in America there." I showed them something I faintly remembered seeing on a Cheech and Chong album cover when I was a kid. They practiced and showed me some of their native signals, a real cultural exchange. They ordered one more round and discussed the recent events of a nighttime soap opera before heading out to another pub, for the "craic," the fun of it. I then found myself sitting with three people I barely knew, a man, James, about my age and his girlfriend, Mary. They were sitting with a friend, Seamus, who was back from London for Christmas vacation, talking about Protestants. "I'm friends with many myself," Mary said. "But they can be a closed lot. For instance, when Catholics throw a party, everyone is welcome. But now when the Protestants throw a party, no Catholics are allowed in. Not one."

"They're different, like," James added. "You'd know one if you saw 'em. They've ruddier cheeks, and the women dress plainer. I can't explain it to you, you just know, that's all. I'm not saying anything by it, one way or the other; I'm just saying they're different. They stick together. I don't mean that in a bad way. But say a Catholic owns a store but the Protestant store across the street has the cheaper prices. The Catholics will go for the cheaper prices; they don't care if the Catholic goes out of business as long as they get a deal, like. Now, the Protestant, no matter what, will always shop in the Protestant store, to help out, you see. They help their own that way.

"Do you mind my asking, which are you?" James asked. "I'm only asking, mind you. It makes no difference one way or the other."

"I was raised Catholic," I said.

"So you're a pagan like me."

There was an uncomfortable silence. It was at this point that it became obvious to me that Seamus was making them uneasy. I got the impression London had changed him. He was handsome and arrogant and he seemed to be trying to prove to them and to me that he was no rube. He told crude jokes and grew more sullen with every drink.

For once I tried to keep the conversation away from emigration. Just as the mood in the pub was disintegrating from raucous to mean, I said goodbye. Out on the street a fistfight had broken out over someone's pregnant sister. As I pushed through the crowd I overheard someone ask, "You mean Hank Williams is American?"

—∿—

While I was filling out papers to renew my visa, Detective Beck came whistling into the barracks and invited me up for a chat in what looked like the interrogation room. As usual, he sat with his parka on to hide his gun, smoking one cigarette after another, each held between his middle and ring finger because his left index finger was mangled with scars.

He explained a few universals about interrogation, how privacy was an important psychological factor, how a generic, unofficial-looking room that had no phone or bars on the windows, or ornaments, pictures, or other distractions, was important; and the trick was you had to appear sympathetic and interested, make them think you were on their side. He leaned back in the chair and looked out the window, where the sun kept going in and out of clouds.

"Although something I've never understood and am afraid of is how after four hours of questions, this big tough guy spills his soul and still thinks he's done himself a favor. I have to wonder, what have I done to him? It's not much different from what you do," he said. "Making people spill their guts." He put one hand over his forehead and pressed his fingers between his eyes.

"If they knew what goes on in my head they'd never give me a gun," he joked.

He leaned toward the window.

"See that man across the street?" A short man in a tweed

cap, raincoat, and dark glasses scurried across the street like a B-movie stool pigeon, glancing furtively at the barracks as he passed.

"He's a criminal," Hugh said, amused. "He's pulled a few heists, but he was just let out on bail because they know he won't break it. He won't because he wants to be able to get bail in the future, you see. For that reason, you can always trust a lifetime criminal like that."

This struck me as typically Irish logic, which got me thinking of the particular nature of Hugh's stories. They had an inertial center, a spiritual and physical immobility—the son in the closet, the nun behind the screen, and aspects of Irish suicide—and then this particular day in what may or may not have been the interrogation room, Hugh told me about his brush with emigration.

It began when his father suggested he become a member of the gardaí. "'Twould be a fine, idle life, my father said. Jaysus, how wrong he was." When he first passed the gardaí exams he told his father he hadn't.

"I finally went to Dublin for gardaí training. There was no way around it. I stayed at a hotel, got up in the morning, had breakfast, packed my gear, and decided then and there to go to England instead of becoming a peeler. I went down to catch a bus to Dun Laoghaire. But I met this young guy standing at a bus stop who was just like myself. He had the usual stamp of the countryman, the suitcases, the tight haircut. I asked him what he was doing. He said he was reporting to headquarters for gardaí training.

"I said, yes, I had almost done that myself but had just now decided to go to England to work on buildings. He said he'd just come back from England. He'd been there for the last six months with the same idea but had found no work. So that was that. I turned right around and went with him to training headquarters. So now, basically, I keep the poor from stealing from the rich."

Hugh had written at least ten resignation letters, but he always threw them away and dreamt of just being on the sea. Unlike his wife, Kathleen, who had traveled all over the world, Hugh had no interest in leaving Ireland. "I love the smell of shit and salt water."

———

I traced Chris Kearnes's and Sarah's lives against local history up to the point where they took different directions. In 1844, the building of the Catholic church was initiated with funds collected in America but delayed during the famine years when fifteen to twenty Roscreans emigrated each day. The church wasn't finished until 1866. In 1892, a fifteen-year-old Irish girl was the first immigrant processed through Ellis Island. One year later, Sarah was born, and Chris was born in 1906, ten years after the first gas lamps had been put up in the streets. The Irish Women's Suffrage Federation had formed by then, and Ireland's population had fallen to about 4 million. At some point they both took the temperance "pledge" to abstain from alcohol, which had been linked with crime and abuse in the home. After the eighth grade, Sarah made lace through a course that was begun in the convent with hopes of mitigating the overwhelming number of women emigrants. In 1912, when Chris was six, Sarah sailed for New York City, not long after all the lime trees in the Catholic churchyard died.

When World War I began and local boys joined up because of a lack of work, mothers from Roscrea protested the war by smashing the windows of the train bound for Dublin. In 1914, they gathered sphagnum moss from the bog to send to France to be used as bandages. In 1918, when Chris was thirteen, her mother died suddenly after a mysterious three-day illness, so Chris left school to help raise her four sisters and one brother until she was well into her twenties. Typhoid broke out in 1922. They lived on porridge, buttermilk, brown bread, potatoes, and peas. "Fuck" was a word she probably picked up from a relative working "for the King's shilling" in the British Army. When one of her sisters ran away to England, deserting her husband and three children, Chris raised them along with the others, while working in the cannery of the meat factory in the 1930s. Electricity was widespread by the time she met Johnny.

"I bore ten, five alive." Chris named them on her fingers, then lost track. "Where did the other two go? I'm sure I have ten . . . too sure of it." Her life had been a hard, sometimes bizarre one. When she was younger, she once took such a violent fall down the stairs she spent a month in the hospital. Just before the fall, Johnny had warned her to stop swearing. "You'll bring the devil into the house."

"Let him come," she said, so after her recovery she was taken to the monastery for a quasi-exorcism just to drive out any lingering bad spirits.

In the meantime, she and her grandmother, Mary O'Reilly, had become inseparable.

———

It was a Tuesday. A drizzling rain was falling across most of Western Europe. And Chris at last began talking about Mary O'Reilly.

"Mary was a terrible woman," she said. "But we had some great sport just the same. She was a terrible woman but she was a great neighbor. Very good-natured. She was good altogether although very cross and contrary."

I held my breath as Chris paused to poke the fire with a stick. She thought for a moment, then continued. "But you know yourself, Joan, you meet some queer people. She was a street angel, house devil, she was."

Mary was, as I learned, also a little more and a little less than a midwife in the days when people still believed TB was a shadow on the lungs.

Chris often accompanied her on these calls, learning about home remedies, at all hours. Newspapers were used as sheets during births. Cauls were considered lucky and sold to sailors to ward off drowning. White and pink achillea were ground and mixed with snuff to relieve headaches; milk mixed with ferret saliva cured the whooping cough; nettle juice, treacle, and whiskey helped lung ailments; and laurel leaves and lard healed burns. Mary also alleviated convulsion in children by dipping them alternately in baths of hot and cold water mixed with mustard.

Mary had knowledge of folk medicine that in another age would have branded her a witch. During the days of the Inquisition midwives were believed to be evil, their deliveries of babies were called "magical baptisms by the kitchen fire." But in her own day, such knowledge was attributed to women known to be "great for drinking." She drank at least two buckets of beer a day. Chris fetched them for her. Mary was once so drunk during confession she passed out and the priest had to drag her out of the confessional. She'd become dangerous and volatile when she was "under the beer." If toys got in her way she'd throw them in the fire, and she once, for reasons that remained a mystery, threw stones at a man on a bicycle.

"From then on," Chris said delightedly, "he put the bicycle away and went to work by walking through the fields, the long way round, so as to avoid her."

Before I came to Ireland, my mother gave me a photo of Sarah—impeccably dressed, her thin arms arched behind her rather vainly. I took the photo, feeling as if I were about to begin the search for a missing girl. For the past few months I'd been visiting the place where she'd last been seen, talking to the people who knew her, following one lead, all the while looking for someone who did not want to be found. For her entire life, Sarah had tried to project this immaculate "lace curtain" Ireland until the myth became like an engram fixed in our genes. Even my mother cautioned me to write only "nice" things about Ireland if only for Sarah's sake.

Given what Chris had told me about Mary O'Reilly, I felt I'd finally found that missing girl or at least the source of her shame—raised in a house that had been condemned, with a mother who terrified everyone around her. Sarah also harbored a lifelong dread of the two properties that most clearly defined her mother—illness and alcohol.

My mother once told me about the time she badly scraped her leg as a schoolgirl. Sarah put a poultice on the wound, but so deep was her dread of pathology, she preferred to ignore its worsening condition, hoping for the best. Even when my mother fell into fever and hallucinations—her little tin soldiers marching around the room—no doctors were called.

And Sarah despised heavy drinkers. As Chris told it, Sarah sent money home every Christmas until one critical year. Mary bought a gallon of stout with the money, then, out of spite, forced Chris to write Sarah that they had "drunk her health." Sarah stopped sending money in her Christmas cards and every year Mary threw these "empty letters" into the fire without reading them.

"After that I never gave myself the habit of writing," Chris said. "Tell me this, Joan. Did Sarah's husband drink at all?"

I told her that my grandfather drank rarely, but when he did, Sarah wouldn't speak to him for days. Chris laughed at this. "I'd be thinking he'd have to snake."

FEBRUARY

I walked up the convent hill and continued along the road with about a three-, maybe four-mile walk ahead of me, having taken up Anthony and Peggy Maher's invitation to come out, although it had been a while since I'd first met the convent art teacher and his wife. A chilling rain had begun hours before, but it was so light it seemed just a sound falling through the hedges along the side of the road, raising an animal sourness out of them.

The Mahers' house sat back from the road at the end of a muddy drive with an acre or so of land that was filled, Peggy told me, with daffodils in the spring. I trudged through the mud to the back door and found Anthony in his garage/studio polishing a piece of black metamorphic rock with abrasive paper. He wore a sheepskin coat, one of those shapeless fishing hats, and had a pipe clenched between his teeth. A drop light hung down over his head, giving the garage a moody glow and casting a circle out around the garage entrance, where a yellow Labrador lay with his head between his paws. Tools lay scattered around the garage, a tungsten chisel, a timber mallet, and a grinding wheel, carbide and carborundum on a shelf against the wall, and, because Anthony sometimes threw his work against the wall in frustration, rock chips crunched under our feet.

"Sculpture has taught me a wonderful lesson in how to be able to accept change. You have to be able to look at something in the cold light of day and say, right, I've gone wrong. You can't put on what isn't there," he muttered, then suggested we go in for tea.

The house was small but warm with a big farmhouse kitchen that was sparse and utilitarian. We sat at the kitchen table with their two daughters, who were bright and chatty. Peggy set a steaming teapot and a plate of scones on the table. The girls beamed with amusement at Anthony as if they expected him to say something outrageous. They tried to embarrass him.

"Listen, Joan, if his students don't behave he makes them kneel in front of him."

He shrugged. "It works. What could be more embarrassing to these girls?"

"And he wears Wellingtons to the bank so everybody will think he's poor."

He frowned at this, much to the girls' joy.

"And he wears pink Wellingtons on the beach!"

He stuck a pipe in his mouth, glowering at them good-naturedly, then sent them off to bed. When Anthony went back outside to tidy up the garage, Peggy whispered to me, "Follow me. I want to show you something I'm not supposed to show to anyone." She guided me through the sitting room, which was crammed with objets d'art and antiques, to an inconspicuous door that opened onto a room that was painted horizontally, half pine green, half midnight blue, the walls streaked with a variety of other colors under a veil of dust. There was a screwless chair, a worktable covered with tubes and coffee cups filled with paint and varnish. On the floor there were rough-hewn chunks of wood, broken hand drills, unfinished carvings, and rejected portraits. Empty frames tilted against the walls and in one corner an anthraxic-looking stuffed squirrel sat on a little wooden perch. The room was as cold and dry and musty as a beehive.

"My favorite is 'The Leper,' " she said, referring to the carving in the library. As Anthony had once explained it, "The Leper" was a memento mori of his experience abroad; he carved it from an Irish yew tree he found on his father's land with all intended irony. "The wood is poisonous, and when the tree was young it was tied together with wire to keep its shape, the wire eating into it over the years and changing its color."

Thomas drove Chris and me out to his house one night. The roads were slick, and as we passed a bog in the watery dusk, Thomas said, "Bogs cause madness. At least, that's what they say." Chris said nothing, looking out of sorts and out of place in the front seat of a car.

By the time we arrived it was dark, but I could see their pony, Pepsi, behind the house and the garage full of turf. Inside, the Kearneses' house had a renovational feel to it, spare furnishings, kitchen windows streaked with black rain. You'd expect to find power tools in the closets, a box of the wrong kind of nails. Crystal golf trophies lined the top of the fireplace, and the television looked unused; the stairs against the wall were too narrow and bare for children to hide on.

We stood in the kitchen for a while to warm up. A "suitor" and his friend had arrived for Eva, Thomas's oldest daughter, a tall, slim girl with translucent skin and deep, ruby-brown eyes. The boys slouched morosely in the corner, elbow to elbow (they wouldn't have seemed out of place in Manhattan's Alphabet City), wearing tattered clothing— ripped jeans, leather coats, bandannas, long hair falling across bad postures, earrings, and military boots. Eva wore Doc Martens and a plaid shirt wrapped around her waist. The funny thing was that everyone, including Eva, ignored the two young men. Thomas referred to them all night as "the creatures," talking in front of them as if they weren't there.

"Look, he brought his bodyguard."

Thomas's mother-in-law, a sweet gray-haired little woman with cat's-eye glasses and a crippling handshake, sat at the kitchen table. (According to Thomas, she once threatened some Jehovah's Witness with a drum of gasoline.) She was playing canasta with his youngest son, an ephemerally pale, blond boy who seemed too shy to leave the kitchen. They had replaced the missing seven of spades with a piece of cardboard and were ignoring it as it passed from hand to hand, just as they ignored the "creatures."

Thomas's wife, Peggy, was pregnant with their fifth child. She alone gave this little scene, the place and the evening itself, a sharper focus just through her quiet pioneer gravity.

Thomas, Peggy, Chris, and I went into the living room and sat in front of the fireplace. Chris fell asleep upright in her chair while we sipped vodka and talked briefly about war and movies, then looked at several decades of photographs—baptisms, weddings, Sunday outings. Once the "creatures" left, Eva and her sister Stephanie played the accordion and keyboard for me, blushing and rolling their eyes, although they seemed secretly pleased to do it.

I mentioned hearing that three years seemed to be the cutoff for emigrants. If they stayed that long they'd stay for life, although some stayed because they were too ashamed to return.

I asked them what they would do if Eva wanted to emigrate. Thomas shrugged, and for the first time that night dropped his intense, old-fashioned parental vigil. "What could we do? We would have to let her go."

———

While having a late-morning scone in a tea shop, I met a woman there who invited me to her home. She was a solid, tough-talking woman with frosted hair and a worldly air. I'd seen her before and overheard her conversation in this same tea shop. Her views had always struck me as conservative but forthright, and I thought we could talk about education and emigration.

As it turned out, she lived just across the street right at the center of town. Inside, the rooms were dark and still. She lit the fire in the living room, which was narrow but lush, but she didn't turn any lights on, so I could barely discern the room or the photographs of her children along the mantel. She seemed tired. She sat on the arm of a chair, then paced suddenly as if against her own will in front of the photos, picking up the same one again and again.

"Hundreds have emigrated that I've known," she said. Her voice was harsh. "We didn't have to go, the people my age. Those who had to weren't highly educated; and if they'd stayed would have ended up on the scrap heap. There wouldn't be room in this small country for full employment. The Irish who are educated are highly educated. It's a much higher standard here. But there are a lot of home problems. Parents don't take an interest and their children don't want to learn and some get left behind because the classes are too big. At one time the rich could buy their way into college, but now it is all done on a very restrictive point system, and grants are meager."

We talked a little bit about Roscrea's restoration, but our conversation seemed constricted, as if she were assuming I was here to talk about something other than what we were talking about, which confused me a little until she handed me the photograph she had kept returning to. The boy in the photo was capable-looking, well dressed, not the sort you see skulking around a snooker table, and then I realized, in one awful moment, that we'd arrived the same day, along the same road. It was a closed casket they brought into the church, but I knew that this "boy" was Jerry Mahir, the young emigrant who'd been living in London and died while vacationing in Denmark.

"He died of complications brought on by asthma. He shouldn't have died," she said, returning the photo to the mantel. "If he'd been here he wouldn't have. I know that. He was very talented, very involved in the music community. A lot of young people today want everything laid out for them. They don't go out and get what they want on their own. My son was the sort to go after his dreams." She held her hands toward the fire, although they couldn't have been cold.

⸺

That chance encounter with the dead emigrant's mother reminded me that for the past few months I'd been trying to understand emigrants in the very place in which they could not be found. Roscrea was embedded in uncertainty and small victories of inaction. It struggled to relate to a world created by the uprooted, and as one confused patriot put it about his future in Roscrea, "I'll get there, wherever there is."

Emigration had exerted a discernible, almost supernatural force on the country and worn down its peculiar strain of people. But modest inferences were inadequate and conclusions hallucinatory. In order to understand the Irish diaspora, I needed to see both sides of the story.

In the meantime, Roscrea was an easy place to leave and it would be an easy place to come back to: I returned my rented typewriter; said goodbye to friends; had one final cup of tea with the Kearneses; and when my housemates bought me one last pint, Anne told me, "You're not bad for a Yank."

The day I left was bright and cold. When I ran into Jimmy Mahoney, who seemed like a new man after his year in prison, he said something that struck me as the truest thing I'd heard so far: "You'd want a sheltery corner and a fire."

NEW YORK CITY:

Four Years Later

JUNE

The tour boat wove through the flat, industrial banks of New York Bay as a tissue of light radiated down between icy breezes and fleeting showers. Most of the passengers crowded inside the lounge for hot chocolate, tilting the boat slightly toward Manhattan and its maelstrom of windows. I was standing alone on the prow watching some mallards float between aircraft carriers.

After leaving Roscrea, I moved with my husband to New York, where we worked odd jobs that were particular to this city—one low point being mousetrapping at a used-book store. After one long, rainy winter I decided to find the neighborhood my grandmother Sarah had lived in and pursue the second part of the emigration story by spending roughly six months—as many months as I spent in Roscrea—learning what kind of world New York was offering the modern Irish immigrant.

I'd heard about Irish women coming to New York in the first half of the twentieth century: one woman believed that all she had to do to talk to her sister back in Ireland was pick up a phone and yell into it without dialing; another thought steam from street grates rose from some eternal fire burning under the city; and another emigrated only because she knew that if she stayed in Ireland her children would move here themselves one day and leave her behind.

I talked to my relatives about Sarah's years in New York, and heard a few details I'd never heard before. After World War II my mother visited the Brooklyn neighborhood where Sarah had lived and learned from an old friend of Sarah's that she'd arrived from Ireland on a June day, traveling in second class rather than steerage to avoid the grueling health inspection at Ellis Island. She took the train to her sister's in Brooklyn, then spent the next six years bouncing from job to job as a domestic servant, a laundress, and a home companion, walking out of a job when it became dangerous or boring. She spent her free time going to movies and Coney Island, playing cards, dancing, and indulging in the latest fashions. When her fiancé from Roscrea was arrested for public drunkenness, she dropped him and began dating a succession of men, sneaking out the back door of restaurants if their conversation failed to amuse her. Unfortunately, my mother couldn't remember the neighborhood Sarah had lived in, just that there'd been a church and the church had burned down.

My Aunt Ceil told me that Sarah had only decided to visit Roscrea for the first time when she was eighty-four years old—almost seventy years after arriving here. "It was psychologically difficult for her to think of going back," Ceil said. "For years she didn't have the money. She really just had to turn her back on Ireland. And by the time she did have the money, her complete separation from the country had become a mind-set." While preparing for the trip, ironically Sarah discovered she was not and had never been an American citizen, something to do with a bureaucratic oversight concerning her husband James's citizenship, which was eventually waived by authorities. But Sarah never voted again.

I leaned over the railing of the prow and looked into the water below, mulling over my plans. Some people came out on the prow and stood next to me. Smoke from vagabond campfires drifted through trees in Battery Park, and as the boat swung out toward the Statue of Liberty, I untied my shoes in case the boat sank. From a distance, I could see Ellis Island with its immaculate, quietly dramatic museum. Across from the museum, however, the island's medical facilities stood in ruins. Once a place where an entire family had been turned away because of one glass eye, it was now like a green plant at night, having no influence and remaining uninfluenced by anything around it as its boards twisted, shrank, and seemed to grow more articulate every year.

The boat turned and headed up the East River, passing under several bridges, then rounding the top of Manhattan, where fires burned in lumberyards along the Bronx shore. When I saw a group of men fishing between drifts of garbage, I was reminded that *The New York Times* once predicted that New York would one day be a place of the very rich and the very poor, those who could afford to stay and those who couldn't afford to leave. In the 1980s, the number of immigrants given legal residence reached its highest level since the decade Sarah arrived here. Like their earlier counterparts, the Irish drifted to cities—Boston, Chicago, Philadelphia, Cleveland—where they were confronted by a sometimes overwhelming velocity and indifference. But for the past two centuries there had been more Irish-born living in New York City than in any other U.S. city.

A young Frenchman and a Texan woman stood talking next to me.

"The Grand Canyon? Why, that's just a little bitty hole in the ground compared to New York City," she informed him, as if New York's proportions were biblical, Jonah's whale about to swallow us all and spit us out a little humbler. The Frenchman thrust his head back and frowned, not so much at what the woman had said as at her choice of fabrics. I leaned even farther over the rail and tried to place the peculiar color of the water. At that moment it seemed that I had only to know the waters around the city to understand the city itself, the East River being this piney-gray hydrography of blue claw crabs, bedsprings, and bad dreams.

Just as the boat crossed the confluence of the East and Hudson rivers, the day drained of what little sun there'd been. As lights flickered on across the cityscape, I remembered something that seemed to capture the whole partnership between immigrants and the evolution of this city: after the ship ballast of shale and coal crossed the Atlantic and arrived here, it was converted into the kerosene that eventually heated the rooms of the immigrants it first help shoulder across the ocean.

Ireland had changed in just the last few years since I'd been there; what I didn't know then was that those changes were reaching inland along the Atlantic coastal plain, urging an epic tradition to run aground.

———

For a while my husband and I lived along a Brooklyn rail line, sharing a large house with an opera singer and a merchant marine. There were bars on the windows; the toilet flushed hot water; and people were routinely mugged on our doorstep. Eventually we moved to the top floor of a limestone row house along a street lined with plane trees—that, as Stendhal put it, "protect the traveler and his dreams." We lived between Green-Wood Cemetery and the elms, sheep meadows, and aquatic turtles of Prospect Park along a ridge overlooking New York Bay. Our subway stop gave us two choices, Coney Island or Manhattan. One day I stood waiting in a crowd for the Manhattan-bound train. On the platform across from us, waiting for the Coney Island-bound train, stood the Tattooed Man, in work overalls, holding a greasy sack lunch—just another workday.

This neighborhood was populated mostly by second- and third-generation Irish, along with a few Puerto Ricans, Dominicans, Koreans, and an Indian newsdealer who called everyone "love." Because the area itself was classically Brooklyn, with that 1950s Catholic ward ambiance, it was flypaper to movie crews, with a largely homogeneous profile of blue-collar families, commuters, artists, and aging Hell's Angels, along with the barroom brawls and bigotry of any small harbor town. Matriarchs in housecoats gabbed on street corners; shelter refugees and drunks gathered at the park's circle drive to drink forty-ounce beers and discuss the day's raw deals; and Boy Scouts camped out in a vacant grass lot surrounded by barbed wire. It was the kind of neighborhood where outsiders found what they thought they'd left behind in their river and factory towns, especially when asked, "Why don't you go back where you came from?"

JULY

On the Fourth of July sulfur clouds hung at clothesline level; policemen supervised illegal rounds of firecrackers, and the gutters were still red with little pieces of rice paper the day Michael Maguire and I met. He was the first immigrant I talked to, and I explained that I liked to spend what I called "documentary time" with people rather than conduct just one cursory interview. He nodded, promising to keep in touch with me. So that first morning we sat in his kitchen under a light that buzzed on and off, drinking the last of his coffee. He looked disheveled and in need of sleep, his face unshorn, dark-rimmed glasses sliding down his nose. His two-year-old son, Simon, sat on the floor driving a toy truck around Michael's bare feet. Michael and Lizzie were both born in Wexford.

"My parents couldn't afford to send me to college," Michael said, sitting as languidly as anyone can on the edge of a chair, with a weary but rather assiduous calm. "And Wexford didn't seem to be a place that I was fitting into."

At nineteen he lived in Dublin, on the dole for two years. Lizzie, who'd graduated from "hotel school," came to work in New York, and Michael, the first in his family to get a passport, followed soon after "with tail between legs."

He had imagined a country of tenderhearted oddballs and spontaneous acts, but when he arrived in the 1980s, America's vinegar was turning to venom, and he found only "cultural squalor."

"I was surprised and still am surprised by the illiberality of America," he said, pausing to suggest to Simon that he not stir our coffee with a pencil. Michael gave me a half-hearted smile, then pushed his glasses up and asked, "Am I explaining all this properly? All the weird juxtapositions? You know, one minute you have *Little House on the Prairie* and you turn the channel and you have the porn channel. It's strange and . . . brain-destroying."

An employment agency gave him a false social security number and hired him out as a temp. After Simon was born in 1993, Michael began freelancing so he could stay home with him. He hesitated, then said, "By the way, we should try interviewing each other at the same time." He wrote a column for *The Irish Voice*, an "Irish in New York" weekly that was founded in 1987 and catered to the new Irish as well as Irish-Americans. The column asked a mix of serious and silly questions, such as "If you were stranded on a desert island with one Irish person, who would it be?" He said he'd turn his address book over to me if I agreed to be that week's subject. I agreed.

"Okay. So, where were we? Oh, yeah. My wife and I have been all over this city in the past ten years," Michael said, sighing. They now lived in the Italian Brooklyn neighborhood of Carroll Gardens. Their apartment was large and airy with toys and baby paraphernalia scattered across the wooden floor, the front room cluttered with a stack of music tapes and books, musical instruments leaning against the walls, and a goldfish circling in a bowl on the fireplace mantel.

"At first we lived in one area which was like living in a small town in Ireland and full of so many things I was trying to escape. Like Sunday mornings after mass, the women go-ing home to make the dinner and the men going off to the bar to drink. Do you know what I'm talking about when I say the Irish drinking? This place was like people coming over here and finding a freedom they never had in Ireland but channeling all that energy into lifting a pint off the bar."

He looked down at Simon, who was untying my shoes. "If you want to draw a metaphorical map, we were running away from all that." Michael swept Simon off the floor and into the next room. He returned after a moment and leaned over the back of his chair, dangling a purple dinosaur.

"Being here has made me more aware of being Irish and it's made me much more open to other cultures, to ethnicity and other ideas. It's not something you think about in Ire-land, but here you're constantly made aware of it." He rolled his eyes and slumped a little bit, tossing the dinosaur to the floor as he sat back down in his chair. "Oh my God. I'm sick of people saying, 'Oh, you're Irish, you guys with your guns and your bombs,' blah, blah, blah."

When I asked him if he'd ever go back to Ireland he thought about it, one hand groping for the handle of his coffee cup, which was empty. "Lizzie and I have become adults here," he said finally, glancing into his cup, then set-ting it back down with a disquiet that suggested that his running had not quite ended. "It would be like going back to a different country. I don't even fit in there when I go back on vacation, and some emigrants who return are treated bitterly because they are successful. On the other hand, Lizzie could come home tomorrow and say pack your bags, and we'd be gone." He paused for a moment, prodding the inside of his cheek with his tongue. "Most people left Ireland, didn't they? Those who didn't, I don't know. I guess they lacked an adventuresome spirit. I think what you'll find is that when the Irish come over here, first they're very suspicious and dismissive and sometimes derisive of Irish-Americans. You know, you're not Irish, what do you know? But I think that as they go out into the world, so to speak, as they become more comfortable in their Irishness, they start to recognize the legitimacy of the Irish-American and to recognize that they *are* Irish.

"I guess I'm becoming Americanized." He looked into the next room, where Simon was now turning the pages of an enormous book. "My son could be President one day . . . God help us."

He jumped up. "Come on." We went into the next room, where he read out names and phone numbers of various Irish he knew in the city, along with warnings about each. "Be careful, she'll want to write the book for you," and "He's a bit of an asshole, but you know, okay."

———

That week the photographer for Michael's column arrived four hours later than I expected. Tall and lanky with a boyish but faintly wrinkled face, he offered no apology, frowning as if distracted by the garishness of his own shirt, which was red and Hawaiian.

It was a hot Friday afternoon. When I offered him a beer he seemed insulted, ultrasensitive to being stereotyped. I sat on my front stoop while he snapped photos of me. When he was done he shifted from foot to foot like a man who'd just had his inner magnet knocked out of him and didn't know where to turn. He explained that he'd spent most of the day trying to take a paparazzo shot of a child star.

"I'm from Dublin all right," he said, "but I don't want to talk about it. *God.* Sometimes I want to go back to Dublin just to get away from being Irish. There you don't have to think about being Irish. Here they never let you forget it." He nervously rubbed his graying buzz cut.

His attitude was my first indication of trouble and the unease I would find among the Irish here, this collective effort to "get away" from themselves, which would baffle and frustrate me for the next several weeks.

When I asked him if I could talk to him more about his experience in New York, he said, "God! It's this whole media thing here, isn't it? Feeding on itself. No, thanks.

"And I can't stand Irish-Americans," he added, then— for whatever reason—archly changed the subject.

"I took mambo lessons to impress this girl . . ." He demonstrated a few dance steps, and from the corner of my eye I noticed a few of my neighbors' curtains moving. He stopped and squinted self-consciously up at the sky, where thunderclouds were gathering. "To tell you the truth, I'm not Irish." He picked up his camera equipment and turned to leave. "I'm South American, and if you ask me any more questions, you'll steal my soul."

———

A few days later I called Michael Maguire, hoping to include his wife in our conversation.

There was a chill in his voice. "What do you want? I thought I answered all your questions."

I explained myself again. He sighed and said, "Try me next month."

———

My list of contacts began to shrink dramatically. One man agreed to talk to me only if the words "Irish" and "Ireland" were never mentioned.

One woman made it clear she despised writers who used description. "You know, when they tell you what the guy's wearing, what he looks like. I hate that."

I crossed off names of anyone who asked, "Will this take long?" or "Exactly how many questions are you going to ask?" Almost everyone said, "Surely you can find someone more interesting than me."

The director of the Irish Immigration Center located in Queens gave me the names of a man and woman. The man, a teacher, stood me up. The woman, on hearing who gave me her name, said, "I'll kill him."

In the four years since I'd left Roscrea, I started to miss it, and I began to see New York in a less than benign light. I felt isolated and ill defined, identifying myself by the restaurant I happened to be in, counting my worth by the number of windows in my apartment, all the while a trespasser on lost ground. I suddenly felt like an outsider here, the Irish reflecting toward me the hostility or malaise they themselves endured or imagined.

Eventually, I came across John O'Mahony. He seemed savvy and candid, and wrote for a gritty tabloid newspaper, which may have been why, in the time it took him to mix a couple of vodka tonics, he apologized for the man he used to be.

"I was pretty naive," he called from his kitchen one late afternoon. I was sitting on the floor in his living room reading his "fax journal," a collection of letters he'd faxed to friends in Ireland when he first arrived in "New Cork"— their nickname for New York.

He came into the living room with the drinks—his plaid shirt and khaki pants accentuating his gray golf-pro looks— then plopped down on the couch and took a quick gulp of his. "These might be a bit strong," he said, flashing me a glance that had no central purpose behind it; it was the glance of a man who moved in several directions at once, afraid to miss anything. His apartment, with its oriental rug, Aztec blankets, and English wing chair, seemed just as agitated.

"The bedroom is air-conditioned," he suggested, referring to the stifling heat, "but you might think it presumptuous of me if I suggested we talk in there."

When he handed me his "fax journal" I thought that at last I'd found someone who would not be timid about the different aspects of his life. I skimmed through them, while he scraped his fingernails with a pen cap and lit one cigarette after another.

The letters contained mostly gossip and breathless appraisals of New York:

> It's a mass of contradictions . . . wild but not as violent as you'd think. I'm totally hooked on black women —their skin, their faces, they're so beautiful.

After a moment, John joined me in reading through the letters, becoming so absorbed by one that his drink stopped halfway to his mouth. "How embarrassing," he groaned, plopping his drink down with a slosh. "Jesus Christ. You're not reading this one." He held it up briefly, then put it in the "too incriminating" pile, which—I noticed with a sinking heart—began to outweigh the letters that I could read.

John was born in Bantry, County Cork, a town of 2,000 people. In the 1970s an American company established an oil-storage depot on its deep-water bay; in 1979 the port became obsolete. The oil company pulled out and the local economy collapsed, forcing many to emigrate. John, who had already decided to avoid the small-town "grind," went to Cork University to study English and philosophy while working summers at a cardboard factory in London to pay tuition and escape the lack of prospects in Bantry.

After graduating he worked at theater companies in London, Belfast, Scotland, and Dublin. He moved back to Cork to head up the regional office of the Irish Arts Council and later in Dublin produced and directed television programs.

"Why did you leave Ireland?" I asked.

He shot me a look of disgust.

"The weather was dreary day after day," he said, one arm flailing. "I just thought: What the fuck am I doing here?" He pointed to my drink, suggesting that I at least try to keep up with him. I sensed he was growing bored and impatient with me and had decided we should just get drunk and call it even. He also began to backpedal away from our subject, putting on an exaggerated brogue as he said, "On the plane

I was crying in me hanky." He laughed and popped a cigarette in the corner of his mouth. "But I'm not an immigrant. My grandfather, who came here in the late 1800s to boomtowns in Arizona and Montana, he was an immigrant. Me? Compared to him, I'm on holiday." He waved the stack of incriminating faxes at me. "We don't have the finality of the old days. I can send E-mail. I can phone. I can be in Bantry in twelve hours."

He lifted his drink, but some new thought again prevented him from taking a sip. "It wasn't as easy as I thought it would be, though," he said. "What you had achieved in Ireland meant nothing here and you had to start from scratch. I was also surprised at the hang-ups of many Americans. Some are fucked up even to the point of lacking common courtesy. For instance, this one woman who interviewed me for a job once wouldn't shake my hand because she'd just had a manicure. Big deal!"

By then we decided to find some cooler air and left his brick apartment building, which overlooked rush-hour traffic along the East River. The temperature was nearing 100 degrees. A haze hung over Queens like the cloud from a thousand clapped erasers. "Even on a day like today," John said as we hopped into a cab, "the weather here is better than Ireland's." I eyeballed him, disbelieving, so John quickly added with a laugh, "At least you get four seasons."

A few blocks later we arrived at a Japanese restaurant. John pulled me through its colorful plastic atmosphere to the back, where a cushioned door opened onto an aquatically lit lounge, which was empty, perfectly chilled, and had silvery blue tones and a harsh film-noir light gleaming from under a neat row of venetian blinds. It was called Angel's

Share, a term that referred to the whiskey lost in evaporation.

"I never set out to be a writer," John said, the vodka having put him in a confessional frame of mind. We took seats at the bar, where two Japanese bartenders washed glasses and grimly nodded at us. "I was like those Irish construction workers who come over here not knowing what end of a hammer to use. Well, I didn't know what end of a pencil to use.

"But the longer I stay here, the more problems I run into, like losing touch with friends. And since my father died my main reason for going back to Ireland has been cut off." He picked up a coaster as if to read it. "I'm a little depressed about that."

Two Japanese transvestites waltzed through the door and primped at the end of the bar as the bartenders hurried over to light their cigarettes.

"See that?" John whispered. "Wild. And here in New York it's the kind of street theater that goes on all the time."

After a drink John suggested we go on. Outside, the copper light of the setting sun tilted across fire escapes, but some kind of equatorial paralysis seemed to have taken hold of the city; guillotines stood outside French restaurants for Bastille Day. We walked a few blocks downtown to the Scratcher (Irish slang for "bed"), a trendy Irish bar with a Galway-in-gaslight mood—polished wood floors, crusty wood tables, and red brick walls. Lou Reed played overhead, votive candles glimmered at each table, and although there was no air-conditioning, the place was filled wall to wall with young Irish writers and artists. There was an earnest heat-defying vitality here as people elbowed back and forth to the bar, becoming ensnared in and disentangled from one conversation to the next.

Immigrants relied on Irish bars for meeting people, cashing checks, and finding jobs and apartments, but they also came for the atmosphere of solidarity and security, which, that evening, was making me feel unwelcome.

I ran into Michael Maguire; he pointedly avoided me and steered his wife to the other side of the room. I ran into his colleague, the paparazzo, sitting at the bar in a yellow Hawaiian shirt, surrounded by a group of fascinated young women.

"How ya doin'?" he asked, also looking slightly put out by my presence here. Neither wanted to talk to me.

After losing sight of John, I talked briefly to a wiry, thick-haired young man who stood brooding in a corner. "You get very patriotic when you move away from home. You miss the auld sod, and the national anthem stirs your blood and all that kind of shit, but if you ask me, financing the IRA isn't being patriotic at all, the way Irish-Americans seem to think it is."

Later, I talked to a group of heavily made-up young women in shiny clothing. After showing off her pierced belly button, one of them pointed out a young man she married a while back so he could get his green card.

"But we're just friends," she yelled over to him. "Aren't we?" He squinted toward her, drunk, trying to place her face. She gave me her phone number. After an hour or so of mingling, John handed me a glass of red wine and yelled into my ear.

"New York is one shit-kicking town. It may be dirty and

frightening but by being here I've lost nothing of the life I had in Ireland. In fact, I've got so much more."

———

A week later I phoned John at his office to suggest another meeting. "Look," he said, sounding tense, "I don't know about this. You're not a very engaging conversationalist, and I feel like I'm talking to a shrink when I talk to you. I mean, I'm just not sure I know what you want from me." Exhausted from explaining my purpose again and again, I finally told him, "Nothing."

I called the girl from the bar—the one who'd married a man so he could get his green card. "Oh yeah, I remember you," she said. "You know what? I was drunk that night. I really don't want to talk to you . . . now or ever."

That night my dreams began to consist of imaginary cities. In one dream, all the houses faced south; in another, animals were frozen to the ground; and in the strangest one, subway entrances stood in the middle of a pine forest. But they all had one thing in common: there were no people. And the message was clear: New York felt empty, and the Irish here seemed robbed of light.

AUGUST

Jenny Brennan lived a few blocks from us. We shopped at the same stores, we used the same laundromat, so I was feeling hopeful about her. One morning we bought some iced coffees and trudged up the hill to her apartment building, talking about various pubs in Ireland, the Galway farm she was raised on, and her struggle during the past five years to make a living as an actress or writer or whatever.

"I don't know what I'm doing," she said. She had reddish-brown hair curling in all directions, straw-colored eyes shades lighter than her tan, and in general a rather sulky quality, as if her beauty were a mistaken invitation to the world. "I can't waitress anymore. I hate it. But I'll manage. Somehow. I don't really have friends left back in Ireland. One is in Denmark. Another is in Germany. People come and go. My being here is hard on my parents. In fact, my mother is quite angry and I don't blame her. There's no reason why I couldn't be broke in Galway instead of broke here in Brooklyn."

She'd acted in a soap opera back in Dublin, but the memory of it horrified her. "I moved to America to escape the shame of it," she joked, then stopped walking for a moment to imitate fans coming up to her on the street: "How are ye, darlin'?" She squealed, pinching her own cheek, then turned her lip up in a mock snarl as we continued walking.

"Actually," she added, "my agent said to go to Los Angeles. But you could die of too much pleasantry out there. New York is the greatest place in the world, although after a while it becomes a small place too."

I asked her about her plans for the future.

"Right now I just want to get back to my air-conditioned room," she moaned, wiping her forehead with the side of her hand.

She lived with her musician boyfriend and her brother, who was studying to take the bar exam, spending all their time in one large air-conditioned room. "The three of us sitting there smoking." She pantomimed smoking a cigarette, hunching over with the snarl back on her lip. "Last night I couldn't even breathe. When I'm up in that room in that air I just feel like my life is over."

We arrived at her apartment, a sunny, rambling place with rooms extending off one long hallway. As we passed the kitchen, she ducked her head in to give it an appreciative glance. "Whenever I'm nervous I make brown bread. It's my therapy. You throw all the ingredients together, then you knead like fuck."

We continued down the hall and into a sparse, barely furnished living room, where she handed me a novel about Northern Ireland. "It's gritty and surreal and bleak," she said, then flopped down in a chair, dropping her chin to her chest as if exhausted by this brief spark of enthusiasm. We sat in silence for a while amid a barrage of heat-related sighs.

Suddenly out of a welter of thoughts she said, "There's a terrible ugliness about the land." I assumed she was talking about the land around us, lost to a metropolitan fugue, but she was referring, instead, to the West of Ireland and the lingering influence of British colonialism, when Irish farmers maintained a save-yourself attitude by encouraging the eviction of neighbors and relatives in the hope of accruing more land for themselves, feeding farm animals while brothers and sisters starved. This turn of mind still haunted the West along with the notion that you don't own land, you belong to it. The attitudes had been hard for her to take, she bluntly admitted.

"But that's what I grew up with." She fanned her face with a magazine and studied the ceiling as if she expected a hole of sunlight to burn through. "Anyway, right now, all I know is I'm being fed."

She promised to call me the next time she made brown bread. She never did, not even to get her book back. My calls to her went unreturned, and I never saw her again.

Maybe it was the heat or my increasingly bad mood, but it seemed then that my life had become hopelessly fragmented. Irish bars had proved fruitless. They were small, impenetrable worlds in themselves. Phones no longer seemed a means of communication but a counsel against it.

———

I escaped to the cool, subterranean vaults of the Transit Museum and browsed through the consoling images of the past, then spent a few days in the solace of documents at the Brooklyn Historical Museum. Its library seemed submerged in a wooden stillness broken only by funnels of light. I pawed through folders of microfiche, these X-rays of Brooklyn's twentieth-century history, reading news and local stories embroidered with the odd details of the times—traveling dentists, dance crazes, elevator operators, and the black-edged envelopes of war dead. I'd begun my search for the church Sarah and James were married in, trying, in the process, to locate the neighborhood Sarah lived in until 1919. This was not a good day for fires, real or archival. For one thing, New York was in its eleventh day of a near-100-degree heat wave; we'd had heat advisories, brownouts; but worse, the Brooklyn Navy Yard was on fire. A far cry from the days when my grandfather sailed between here and Cuba—when sailors walked arm in arm and the waterfront was lined with saloons—the yard was now an industrial park surrounded by concertina wire and housing projects, and for the past thirteen hours its ivy-covered yard had been pouring a cancerous plume of smoke across the horizon. The library was airless and empty except for me and two Hasidic Jews, who looked dressed for an unending winter.

Eventually I found a five-alarm fire that burned a Brooklyn Catholic church in the 1950s, and as I wrote down the address, it occurred to me that some families leave ashes where others leave paper trails.

——

A few days later I walked down to the church—St. Stephen's—taking a street that began at the edge of Prospect Park and continued downward through prosperous areas of stolid old brownstone before bottoming out along the Gowanus Canal. The canal, which flushed debris from gravel yards and foundries, was always an oil-on-velvet green in an area where German shepherds roamed rooftops and garage mechanics stood around garbage can fires in the winter. But the old brick factories, neon signs, and casket companies soon merged into Carroll Gardens, a forty-block area once considered a part of Red Hook. When Sarah lived here, most of her neighbors had been Irish and German, all gradually giving way to an influx of Italian dockworkers and Syrians. In the 1960s, this expanse was renamed by real estate agents for Charles Carroll, the only Roman Catholic to sign the Declaration of Independence. This was Michael Maguire's neighborhood, a place for those "running from their Irishness."

I lived in this quiet residential neighborhood myself one summer before graduating from college. My friends and I would sit on the roof and watch flocks of trained pigeons dive through the air around St. Stephen's steeple. We danced; we went to Coney Island; and every morning ship horns and the clang of bell buoys drifted up from the shore of the Buttermilk Channel, where two enormous white warehouses sat along the water like tribunals of oceanic law. There were pastry shops, bakeries, brownstones, and sidewalks lined with generous shade trees. Rich with festivals, yeasty inhabitants, and the occasional public dispute—"Get in the fuckin' car, Rita"—its Old World atmosphere fell just short of quaint.

As I walked through the neighborhood that day, swings in the park creaked in the wind and dust whirled up in little funnels from the basketball courts; old men in a boccie ball pit stood holding caps down on their heads, laughing, and two elderly women in matching housecoats watched me pass without looking directly at me. The core of the neighborhood had never changed even as its edges had unraveled, as buildings were torn down and highways put in, street names changed and addresses altered.

Two of Sarah's older sisters—Maggie and Chris—came to New York and to this neighborhood ahead of her. Maggie settled down with a family, while Chris found New York unlivable, returning to Roscrea almost immediately. It was Maggie who eased the transition to life here for Sarah, and Maggie who met a sailor named James in Central Park, inviting him for Sunday dinner to meet Sarah. In 1918, Maggie died from influenza, one of 12,000 New Yorkers to fall to this epidemic. Knowing that Sarah would be expected to move in with her husband and raise her daughter as her own, on her deathbed Maggie urged Sarah to avoid this, to marry James instead and start her own life. But deathbed wish or not, Maggie's widowed husband did expect Sarah to do the customary thing and, in fact, insisted that Sarah also marry his brother to make the situation more seemly. Sarah refused the offer. Her brother-in-law broke all ties with her, and the unknown fate of her niece haunted Sarah her entire life, remaining her one lifelong regret.

When I found St. Stephen's Church I wondered if Sarah would recognize it, sitting as it did along the highway that had exacerbated the waterfront's decay. Paint peeled off its sides; the roof was covered with pigeon feces; and—a remnant of the fire—its windows had been replaced, not with stained glass, but with wood boards, which gave it a withered facade. The fire itself hadn't originally made the papers but had become "news" only when the church was rebuilt with the help of Protestants and Jews.

Inside, the church air smelled of crayons, and there were saints that would have been unfamiliar to Sarah—St. Bartholomew brandishing a meat cleaver, a blind St. Lucy. Like the neighborhood itself, the church had transformed from the austere to the operatic, new saints replacing the old.

—⁓—

The heat wave continued: dogs panted outside smoke shops; car fumes and dust revolved overhead, and water mirages undulated over two-lane avenues. The planet had reached its farthest orbit from the sun the day I set out to reach the waterfront. As I stopped to pump up the leaky tires of my five-speed Raleigh bicycle, an upstir of pigeons erupted in front of our local armory. This massive castlelike garrison, which was built in part because of social turmoil among immigrants, was now a homeless shelter, an overpowering edifice to hold the defenseless. I continued cycling as the pigeons resettled behind me, and crossed over a highway, then along the edge of the cemetery. It was an immaculately groomed woodland where the Manhattan skyline rose out of the tombstones like the crypt of the world's most arrogant dead man. The last time my husband and I walked through the cemetery we discovered a colony of wild green parrots living in the trees. After acclimating to North American winters, several parrots had been spotted in Long Island over the past ten years, an incongruity that reminded me of Ireland's palm trees.

I passed a train yard and a hillside of apartment buildings which merged into a neighborhood of neat row houses and church steeples. For a few moments, I followed the ridge paralleling the harbor, looking for a street that ran uninterrupted to the water. The streets carved through Brooklyn like fossil indexing, each environ preserved in the particular decade in which its economy had stalled. I chose a street and began to coast downhill as one era peeled away from the next every few blocks: the brownstone and limestone from the days of fortune; the brick row houses from the days of hard labor; and the pink and blue aluminum siding from the days of the "hard sell." Closer to the water, along the washout of Brooklyn's glacial ridge, conditions became strictly Depression era: a few narrow houses covered in moldering tar paper and tin roofs and empty lots glittering with broken glass.

Immigrants and industry were inextricable in the days when Brooklyn fed, clothed, and provided building materials for the Midwest as fast as the Irish and their fellow immigrants could lay down and spike the tracks that took them there. Between 1910 and 1920, 124,000 Irish moved into Brooklyn. This cheap labor stoked the country's economy, introduced new strains of corruption and violence into the underworld, and forever altered its political, artistic, and religious terrain. Industrial expansion didn't stop until after World War II, when the Brooklyn Navy Yard closed and factories relocated.

At the end of the twentieth century, Irishness in America seemed to have reached its saturation point. Newer and deeper influences were coming from other parts of the world—the Caribbean, Central America. I began to see the new Irish almost as icons, a population, once driven along by its own weight, now sensing the awkwardness of its own discontinuity.

I continued coasting downward. A brilliant white ocean liner filled the horizon between a narrow prospect of gas stations and bodegas. By then, my front tire was making a funny rubbery sound again, but I kept going, winding my way through a slow-moving string of cars under an elevated expressway. At sea level, the water disappeared from sight behind piles of gravel. I passed an enormous yellow detention center, a group of Hispanic women and children lined up at its door. Most of the detainees inside were immigrants awaiting possible deportation, and, as if to bear this out, the building was surrounded by suicide netting. On the other side of the center there was a smudgy road bound by old creosote telephone poles and a dozen or so warehouses twelve stories high with droopy electrical wiring and paint peeling off windowsills; the seams of a railroad track emerged through the tar and brick of the road, and workers in gray overalls sat in groups on cement abutments eating lunch, looking spectral in the midday sun. A half dozen German shepherds roamed through tall weeds growing up around a tiny aluminum diner, and at the end of this road a merry little ice-cream truck jingled around the parking lot of a strip club.

There used to be a coaling road along here that linked Brooklyn's entire waterfront. One October day in 1958, two blocks of it collapsed and slid into the sea, marking the end of an era. But now that this expanse was truly marginal the street itself had disappeared under an enormous parking lot filled with demolished police cars parked under a lethal glare of light. I pedaled passed this compound, then turned down a cement pier. A boatload of harbor police were motoring in from the bay. I waved; they waved back. Farther out along the pier, I came across an abandoned little carnival. Its tiny Ferris wheel creaked in the wind, and its child-size boats and rockets were mired in drifts of sand. The piers, which were slowly being eroded by aquatic worms, had "Do Not Go Beyond This Point" signs posted on them, but I ignored them, determined to get as close as possible to what muck-rakers used to call the Pool.

Clearly, progress now meant contraction. We'd gone from pneumatic tubes to faxes, massive machinery to beams of light, and this was nowhere more evident than along the Brooklyn shores, where the docks and piers lay near collapse like skeletons along the floor of a drained lake. The harbor looked flat and as colorless as a flooded quarry. The water smelled faintly of vinegar, and on the pier across from me, two Dominican boys fished, happily shouting back and forth to one another with the ghosts of rain puddles at their feet.

—⁓—

"You get old fast in this town," Tom Weir told me, holding the door open as we emerged from the byzantine corridors of the Brooklyn Academy of Music, where he was spending his last week as its design coordinator. Some people I'd met at a rooftop party suggested I call Tom. "He won't let you down," they assured me.

As we walked through lunch-hour traffic, searching for a place to eat lunch, he told me that BAM was built in this neighborhood because many decades ago the area promised to be the cultural center of the world. "But as you can see . . ." He gestured toward these now indistinguishably urban streets that bristled, not with energy, but with something more like the last trembles of its fall from grace— furniture stores, military recruiting centers, liquor stores with hand-painted signs, and a chop suey restaurant that looked as if it had shut its doors while *The Honeymooners* was still on the air. This peripheral area was now marked by open static spaces, fences, surplus stores, and the Williamsburgh Savings Bank tower—like an obelisk to hard-boiled detective novels.

Pedestrians stood on corners looking away from each other, but Tom, who had deep laugh lines in an otherwise youthful face, maintained a resilient patience toward the streams of people around us. But then, there also seemed less of Tom for the world to crush. In fact, the only hint that the sun affected him at all was when we stepped inside a Caribbean fast-food restaurant and looked at the menu of cow feet, goat roti, and fish tea. Exchanging disheartened looks, we ordered ginger beers, then headed for a booth. He was, in fact, open and enthusiastic about talking to me, but, unfortunately for me, after three years in New York his life was about to take a curious turn: he and his wife, Marion, a Chicago-born actress, were going to have a baby in Ireland—where the health care was free—then return to New York after the baby was born.

"Right now," he said, tossing his head toward the glare of the window, "Ireland seems idyllic."

Tom, thirty-four, had a fairly typical middle-class suburban childhood. He studied math and philosophy in college, graduating in the mid-1980s during the first great wave of emigrants. But while 80 percent of his class left for London or New York, Tom stayed and worked for eight years as the curator of the college's gallery for contemporary art.

"A good job, but then, of course, it was a prison as well," he said. "I was twenty-eight and still hadn't left the campus grounds, so one day I just threw it in and vowed I'd never stay longer than three years at any job." He foundered for a while before finding two jobs, one setting up a computer animation program at an art college and the other opening gallery space for a community arts center, where he developed "playful" installations along the docklands with the help of artists and women and children from the slums.

One of the few of his generation who'd initially stayed in Ireland, Tom had been considered a weirdo.

"We viewed returning emigrants with great amusement," he said. "Christmas Eve we'd walk up and down Grafton Street because that's where everyone who got off the plane would be. You'd see someone doing the London yuppie thing or somebody who'd been in Texas and he comes back huge in this Orson Welles suit."

But Dublin eventually "closed down" for him too.

"I went to the travel agent and for some bizarre reason I wanted to go to Bali." He said the word as if this Indonesian island were some kind of wildly outdated fashion trend. There were no immediate flights to Bali, so he flew to New York instead, where he slept on a friend's floor, worked at NYU setting up an exhibition, and bartended the opening night of a trendy Irish East Village hangout. That night he met his wife-to-be and witnessed his first American riot, as policemen chased Tompkins Square anarchists down the street.

"Unfortunately I felt pretty disillusioned by the whole New York art scene," he said. "To be a curator and to do anything in an interesting personal way you have to know the culture. I'll give you an example. At NYU, for the opening of the Ireland House, an artist with a Loyalist Belfast background set up a pair of satellite dishes. On one side he had a picture of a broken heart, and on the other side a photo of this woman crying. Her fiancé had been killed by the IRA and she had committed suicide a week later. Americans weren't getting it, you know, and the NYU president said they had to come down. That was my first inclination that this wasn't my turf. The notion of Ireland here isn't something I have access to. Americans are conceiving of another place entirely." He shrugged. "I guess they wanted a little leprechaun on a shamrock."

His father died while he and Marion were still dating, so she flew to Ireland with him. "She came to the house and met my mother and we were sitting with the coffin when my mother said to her, 'You know, the first time I met my husband's mother was sitting beside his father's coffin.'" Marion and Tom returned and were married upstate by a justice of the peace.

A group of women entered the restaurant bringing in a blast of hot, stale air; Tom fanned himself with his hand and laughed. "What I'm really looking forward to is a sense of time. In Ireland, you have a midmorning, you have a late morning, an early afternoon, late afternoon, and so on. Here it's a.m. . . . p.m.

"Oddly enough I do feel anchored in both Dublin and New York. When I met Marion I immediately wanted to apply for citizenship and vote. I'll miss New York. Nothing's assumed here, whereas in Ireland, you're either Catholic or lapsed Catholic. Last time I was in Ireland I had a great time, but when I came back to New York it was like, ah yeah, I know why I live here. You need that grit under your skin."

As I walked back to the subway I found myself comparing Tom with other Irish immigrants I'd met. Tom, who seemed more connected to and less troubled by America, also better understood my interest in the modern Irish experience. To him I was not just some snooping Yank. His wife was American, so he was able to see how ties to the "old country" were an integral part of the American consciousness. And his children and his children's children would be raised in America, so he understood that my interest sprang from—whether she liked it or not—something instilled by my grandmother.

In the meantime he left for Ireland, and I never saw him again.

———

For weeks the sound of a pile driver's relentless pounding had been drifting up from the harbor, and a parrot in the courtyard behind our apartment had been squawking throughout the long days. I might have seen both of these as lending the summer a certain cinematic resonance, but, against the silence of my phone, I could see them only as ill omens.

In order to forgo my expectations about Irish immigration, I needed to examine the relationship between the new Irish and their forerunners. The Immigration Act of 1965 limited Irish immigrants because they'd been unable to prove that they were political refugees or that—because Irish immigration had dropped after World War II—they had close family ties here. Since this effectively curbed the once continuous influx of Irish, it wasn't until the 1980s, when the Irish began slipping into the country illegally, that the stream reunited with itself. By then there was not only a generation gap but a gap between the old, rural, agricultural Ireland and the new, urban, industrial Ireland. Immigrants who came in the 1950s and 1960s were generally less sophisticated, with limited education. They found the new Irish to be insolent, wanting everything handed to them, unwilling to work their way up from the bottom. But, at the same time, the new Irish energized languishing Irish neighborhoods, providing revenue and labor, and creating a mutually exploitative situation—the older Irish as employer, the younger as employee. Still, the new Irish adhered to one another within the larger, generic community, finding the older Irish and Irish-Americans too conservative, too all-American. The older Irish and Irish-Americans, who had more in common with one another, found the new Irish too European. With rare exceptions, most Irish never saw the "true" America and sneered at anything outside of New York City. America and Americans—me—had become an imposition, a reminder of their disillusion and their discovery that the dream is not a place, and that the nature of the planet is unchangeable: the moment you turn your back on a place you must face it from a different direction.

As one Irish-American put it: "They're not my kind of people. They're also very prejudiced against immigrant groups. I mean, they even seem to hate themselves."

The modern world required a fresh response, and the new Irish had been prepared for this via a different medium—television instead of letters, although both could be equally ambiguous and misleading. The new Irish were less sentimental about their native land, and less impressed by America, taking a more guerrilla approach to it—get in, get what you can, then get out. In many ways they reflected the current American way of life. And because assimilation was not instantaneous—as some clearly hoped it would be—it became a point of resentment and was rejected as an unworthy aspiration. The Irish, like all displaced people, seemed to be blaming the disorder of their lives on their surroundings, and this was the bent frame of mind I was battling.

I spent one sizzling day in a wicker chair by a hotel pool overlooking Central Park, as recommended to me by a former Miss Ireland. A warm breeze came through an open window. Children splashed in the shallow end, and old men, who looked as if they'd just stepped off a Lucian Freud canvas, gingerly dipped their toes into the water. I'd met Miss Ireland in a midtown bar one evening. She'd breathlessly described her multiple successes in life and how she'd taken to modeling like "a duck to water" and so on.

"I'll just keep talking," she warned me, and she had for a full hour on how America was her kind of place, how New Yorkers were "honest to God people" and the importance of having "buckets" of money and living in Beverly Hills one day. My thoughts wandered as she talked, thinking about how in Ireland I'd been treated like a person, whereas here I was being treated like the media. At one point she tapped my tape recorder. "Is this thing on or am I just rambling here?"

She had few complaints about life in New York except for the price of cornflakes and Harlem: "If I were poor, I'd have a humble little cottage in the country somewhere and at least have some dignity."

SEPTEMBER

For Brona Crehan it had been the leaving more than the going. I couldn't recall how we'd met, but she occasionally gave me tickets to the Irish Repertory Theater and lent a sympathetic ear to my complaints. It was the second time we spoke that, over the course of the evening, she began to slip into the past tense, referring to New York not as if she were living here but as if she had lived here once upon a time. Raised in Dublin, she had found Ireland disheartening and parochial. "Do you remember the story of the bishop of Galway with the seventeen-year-old son in America? He fled the country suddenly and the next day at mass when there was no sign of him, the congregation asked each other what was going on. Somebody said he's gone and they asked, you mean he's dead? And they said no, worse."

She laughed, but Brona had a certain wistfulness about her, a spare melancholy. When I arrived at her Upper East Side walk-up apartment, she was standing at the entry of her kitchen sipping a can of beer. Tall, with dark eyes and a tanned seraphic face, she was wearing a black skirt, a white blouse, and slippers over her panty-hosed feet.

"Since I've been here my salary has doubled," she said. "I could have banged my head against a brick wall for a million years and that wouldn't have happened in Ireland." These days she did a lot of traveling for her work as a perfume company's executive assistant and sang in clubs when she could. In fact, I'd caught her backup musicians in the middle of a rehearsal. Patrick and Brian were both first-generation Irish. Patrick told me his parents came from Waterford to Brooklyn and that when he was a child they took him to visit an old woman who had been a matchmaker for everyone who came from Waterford to New York.

The phone rang and Brona picked it up. "I'll call you back. We're having a practice."

"What are you practicing?" Patrick called out.

"Shut up," she said, laughing, as she hung up the phone. "You'll get me in trouble."

There were various guitars, a tin whistle, and a mandolin scattered around the room. The guitar that Brona's father had bought her when she was young leaned in the corner.

He once told her, "It's not really where you are but who you're with." But because of the summer heat, the guitar was now too warped to be played.

"I remember my first year away. I couldn't wait to get back to Dublin," she told me. "I just lived for going back. Then, when I was home, it wasn't what I thought it would be," she said. "A typical case of the faraway hills are green. Nobody had changed, everybody was doing exactly what they were doing when I left. Emigration can't be good, but I'm always glad to leave Dublin. Who wants the dampness seeping into your bones?"

She came to New York on a whim and loved it immediately. "But at one point I was also wondering: What the hell am I doing? I'm twenty-five, starting all over again, making new friends, doing things I don't want to do, but what's the alternative? Eventually, I hope to meet somebody, get married. If he's American, I'll stay here. If he's Irish, I'll go home."

Her parents lived in France, so, as an idea, "home" had become that much more ambiguous.

"I felt such a sense of freedom in New York. There was nobody there to pass judgment on you."

The air conditioner, which overlooked an air-shaft alley, plinked and creaked with residual winds from a Carolina hurricane.

"If I'm ever rich," Patrick was saying, "and have roadies . . ." Brona and Brian exchanged amused looks that momentarily silenced Patrick.

It was late, but everyone decided to have one more beer rather than go out into the torrential rains. We told jokes, talked about music and dating. Patrick's girlfriend had just broken up with him, and, as if to prove it, he kept breaking into George Jones songs all night. Brona announced she had a date the next night.

"I've had some minor setbacks, been dumped," she said, laughing at the bluntness of the word. "Most American men I've known have been Irish-American, so they're wise to us. But I prefer Irishmen. My grandmother always said the devil you know is better than the devil you don't know."

———

I stopped for tea in an East Village Irish coffeehouse one late afternoon. It had dirty brown walls covered in warped music posters and candles burned in the windows. Two Jamaicans in full dreadlocks had just ordered pints of Guinness and a young Chinese couple sat gazing raptly at one another. A handful of young Irishmen sat around a group of tables. One of them, with his head shaved bald, was stamping dates onto concert posters, looking both harried and smug. The street outside the window bristled with obnoxious energy, and when a punk panhandler walked past the door—all spiked hair and spray-painted leather—the bald man shouted at him, "Get a room at the Chelsea." The punker, without missing a beat, gave us all the finger.

Two men across from the bald man rolled cigarettes and drank beer while a big white dog slept restlessly at their feet. A fourth man, who'd been reading a tiny paperback, suddenly looked up and announced he was going "home" for three weeks.

"Lucky bastard."

"Bring me back some chocolate."

The waitress brought a tray of beers to their table, then

lit a cigarette, her eyes fixed on the frenetic activity outside. The bald man looked up at her. "I'm working my ass off here," he informed her. She sent a stream of smoke toward him along with a callous look, then said, "Now you know how your ancestors felt."

When I returned home that day I took a deep breath and phoned Michael Maguire to see if he had time to talk.

"We're moving back to Ireland," he told me, in a tone that suggested I was responsible for this with all my questions. I asked if I could talk to him and his wife before they left. "That's . . . no . . . that's not possible." Then he hung up with barely a farewell.

———

One day I talked on the phone to Sinead Kirwan, the young woman in Roscrea who'd described Ireland as "the green land going away."

After giving the Bronx one more try—holding down three waitressing jobs for a while and taking a few business classes—she'd returned to Roscrea only to find that she felt like a stranger there. She moved to Dublin and began working at a tax-free shop in the Dublin airport, where the world now came to her weary with travel.

She gave me her Aunt Theresa's phone number and a few days later I was walking down an el-darkened street to visit Theresa, heading toward the apartment building where she and her husband, Pat, were superintendents in the part of the Bronx that had "suffocated" Sinead.

I had just passed the Terminal Bar when an aureole of sun broke over the rooftops, casting surrounding apartment buildings in an orange glow. Summer still clung to these broad gummy sidewalks and the air smelled of fried chicken and camp toilets. Like a lot of New York neighborhoods, this one had emerged as a sort of commercial purgatory: strip malls and chain stores for meat, dry cleaning, bagels, bin goods, "bargains," OTBs, H & R Blocks, and the International House of Pancakes. Auto-part shops and funeral homes looked interchangeably municipal; every bar had a neon shamrock in the window, and because of the shadows under the el, store lights flickered on here hours before the rest of New York prepared for night.

In the 1960s, with the influx of drugs, Irish, Germans, Italians, and Jews began their "white flight" from the South Bronx, some pushing into areas like this one. There were still a few hangers-on, like Theresa and Pat. When they arrived the area was a "stable" neighborhood of predominantly working-class Irish. In the 1970s, when sex education was brought into the schools, more conservative Irish left a gap in the population. Now, those who stayed were yielding more and more of this narrow basin to African-Americans, Arabs, and Hispanics, who were themselves intent on getting out of the South Bronx.

Theresa's building was located in a colony of red brick apartment houses under a ragged assembly of fire escapes and TV antennas.

When I joined her and her friend Mary, they had just cleared the dinner dishes in the dining room.

"You're in the writing business?" Mary asked, laughing. "We were expecting an old lady, weren't we?" Mary had whitish-blond hair, a drawn face but a playful note in her voice, eyes hidden behind thick lenses. Theresa poured wine for her. "I won't be able to drive home if you give me any more wine," Mary protested, moving her glass closer to the bottle.

Theresa, who had four children, was slim with a flat nose and wide thick lips; she wore sunglasses on her head secured by a gold chain, and had that quiet, baffling self-doubt that women of her generation sometimes had. She and Mary spoke between each other's hesitations as if waiting to be contradicted by the other. When I complimented Theresa on her crystal wineglasses, she said in a low monotone, "Someone asked me the name of these glasses once. And I said, 'You know, I'm lucky my kids have names, much less my glasses.'"

The dining room was wood-paneled. There was a china cabinet filled with mementos of varying worth. A few modern religious icons hung on the walls and golf clubs and a panful of coins sat in one corner. A baseball game played on TV in the next room, and every now and then street noises broke in—sirens, the squeals of Puerto Rican children playing on the corner, and a Latino beat thumping from a passing car.

"My aunt married a guy," Theresa said, resuming a conversation about fate they had begun before I arrived. "They were walking home together and one of them lit a match to light a cigarette and that was the only look she got of him."

"And she married him even after closer inspection?"

Mary mumbled something about getting back home to walk her cocker spaniel, but Theresa insisted she stay to "verify" the course of her fate.

Theresa was born in a town not far from Roscrea. "Family life was good but we were poor. I spent many a day in the bog working." She quit school after the eighth grade and waitressed until her uncle offered to pay her way to the States. "The United States meant lifestyle, wealth. I wanted to see the other side, to explore. My mother was heartbroken. The night before I left was like a wake." She looked at Mary for confirmation.

"In those days when you left," Mary said, nodding, "it was like you didn't know when they'd see you again."

When Theresa emigrated from Ireland at nineteen she didn't, as had become the norm, take an airplane. Her father, a blacksmith, accustomed to working with iron and fire and water, believed that airplanes shouldn't by rights "stay up in the air." So, after no one questioned the ability of tons of steel to float on the surface of water, Theresa traveled by ship.

"I'm getting lonesome just thinking about it again," Theresa said, smashing out a cigarette and settling back in her chair. " 'Twas a foggy morning in Cobh and you could hear the ship's horn blowing. It was lonesome altogether. I'm on the tender waving. I wasn't crying until this guy beside me who was half bombed was singing 'and I never more roamed my own native home, Tipperary so far away' . . . and then I bawled." She paused, a wistful smile on her face. "It was a wonder looking out at the ocean." When they docked at Thirty-third Street, the transformation began from Theresa's visions of wealth and glamour to the reality of hard work and isolation.

"Oh my God, how stupid I was. I remember I saw some spit on a railing, and I said to meself, I didn't know they'd have spit in America!"

She stayed with her aunt and uncle for a while and

worked various jobs, from department stores to housework and waitressing. Now she worked part-time as a receptionist.

"In the old days we always had an active house. The Catholic school was right here and if the kids needed a drink of water or a Band-Aid 'twas here they came."

The phone rang. Pat, who'd been watching the game in the other room, picked it up. A retired bus driver, he had a strong symmetrical face and wore thick black eyeglasses.

"That might be my daughter," Theresa said excitedly. "She's in the Cayman Islands and has just decided to live there."

"It's the deacon," Pat said, and then into the receiver, in reference to me, "You better get down here, Deacon, you're missing the show."

If Theresa hadn't met Pat, and if it hadn't been for the fact that he could not have found steady work in Ireland, she would have left the United States long ago. They'd seen too many changes. Pat had been robbed a few times while driving the bus, and their son, after five years as a cop in the South Bronx, had to quit due to emotional distress; a baby had died at his feet after being thrown from a window. The area had gotten "very noisy" and was no longer a place that attracted young Irish; in fact, a future here now seemed about as implausible as air flight.

"If the young come here," Theresa said, "they better themselves quickly and move to the suburbs before they get stuck in a rut. And Ireland itself is changing. What with the church being exposed for its hypocrisy, the changing attitudes, it's becoming a more acceptable place for young people, who, if they can stay, do.

"We go back for summers, but every time I leave Ireland I'm heartbroken all over again."

There was a lull in the conversation, during which both Theresa and Mary looked down at the table as if it were stolen property.

"You know what I find when anyone comes from Ireland?" Mary said eventually. "Everybody goes out of their way to be nice to them and will do anything for them. But it's not like that when you go back to Ireland. They resent us."

"I found that too," Theresa agreed. "We're from America, so to them we have plenty and we are supposed to give back to them."

On that note, Mary gave the table a light slap and rose to go.

"I'll walk you to your car, then," Theresa insisted.

"I'm not afraid."

"Do you want some homegrown tomatoes?"

"I have my own. I'll call you when I come back from the beauty parlor."

"Now, don't get your hair cut too short. The way it is now is nice."

"I'm going to Ireland for three weeks," Mary explained to me, patting her stomach. "But how fat I am."

"Oh, get out of here," Theresa said, laughing in exasperation.

It was getting late, and Theresa was concerned that I should get on the subway and out of this neighborhood soon. We walked into the hall. Their apartment consisted of a series of oddly fitted rooms, each blocked off from the other, but this provided a sense of privacy rather than congestion.

The kitchen was a narrow path that ended at an unfinished wooden wall and reminded me of horror movies where the heroes have boarded themselves up against some unspeakable mayhem. Generally, the apartment conveyed mixed intentions: its inhabitants hadn't quite arrived but they would never leave.

"I thought you were doing the dishes for me," Theresa teased Pat, who was staring indecisively into the refrigerator. Another car thumping a Latino beat passed by, shaking some glasses on the counter. "It's just a different culture," Theresa said, "and I feel like the minority now. The crime rate has gone up and there's more noise and congestion. But they're good people just as they are. Being here has broadened my horizons. In Roscrea you'd be looked down on if you weren't born on the right street."

Both Pat and Theresa walked me outside.

"I guess we could go back at any time," Theresa said. "But now that I have grandchildren here I couldn't leave. Anyway, I think where you're happy, that's where you belong."

On the corner they gave me directions, hastily interrupting and finishing each other's sentences in an effort to get me safely out of the neighborhood.

"Good luck now," Pat shouted against the noise of the streets.

OCTOBER

I'd been talking to the New York Irish for months but felt no closer to understanding their mood. Coming here in the 1980s had not only been wise but necessary. But news of change in Ireland had been trickling into conversations. The Catholic Church's grip on the country was loosening; the economy was improving. In an Irish bar one night one young woman said this about it: "Yes, things are getting better there, but it's not *brightening*." It seemed vague. She seemed vague. The truth was, many didn't know why they came, just that it had always been expected of them. Brian Doyle was different.

We were drinking coffee in a West Village cafe— crushed-velvet cushions, Victorian floor lamps. Men sat at marble-top tables discussing such subjects as architecture and trust; waiters in white aprons leaned against the wall, their arms folded, heads together in hapless conversation. With his imprint of the working class, Brian seemed a little out of place here. He was ghetto-thin with rugged, unshorn features. His brown eyes were deep-set and had a look in them that shifted between treason and cheerful resignation. As an Irishman, a Catholic, and a homosexual in equal parts, Brian had earned his sleepless nights.

"It was a relief to get out of that awful goddamn country," he said.

Homosexuality had only just been decriminalized in 1993, but gays marched in Dublin's St. Patrick's Day parade without controversy, an irony that seemed to typify the difference between the Irish and the Irish-Americans.

He'd been raised in a housing estate where sickness and religion "colored" his entire life, from the celiac deficiency he was born with—marked by malnutrition—to his current fear of AIDS—marked by funerals.

"My mother would beat the shit out of us but"—he smiled crookedly and rubbed his arms—"but nothing abu-

sive. It was the nuns who gave me all this maternal tender-
ness that my mother never had time for, and I immediately
connected with them and wanted to be like them. Obvi-
ously, I couldn't become a nun, so I became dedicated to
becoming a priest. Many of the men drawn to monastic life
were probably gay," Brian said, gesturing dramatically. "We
have evidence of this in poetry, but we have been denied
our own history. To me, anyone who refuses to deny who
they are is a saint. Like Oscar Wilde. I grew up in the 1960s,
only reading about the changes happening in the rest of the
world, like the sexual revolution."

When he was thirteen, he trained to become a Christian
Brother.

"It was madness, because I had soon become my own
worst nightmare, everything the Brothers lectured against. I
was always getting bashed up and beaten, but I'd always say,
'This is God's will, this is a part of being a saint.' "

In 1981, he studied theology at Maynooth, then decided
to continue his education at St. John's in the States.

"When I first came to the West Village I felt like a kid
in a candy store. The bars never closed, so, Jaysus, you could
sit there all night manipulating the stereotype. I'm Mick.
I'm Paddy. I'm Jack. I used to literally run back and forth
between this gay bar and this Irish bar in a single night. I
was in such conflict about who I was."

As he put it, he'd only managed to make a "geographic
escape" from Ireland, as if his soul were still back there enduring all sorts of Boschian horrors. "Some people would
have you believe that I belong to one of the coldest races
on the planet."

He glanced out the window at the brick buildings across

the street where late-day shadows pushed a soft autumn light up toward the rooftops. Pamphlets gray with sneaker treads flapped in the streets and incense smoke curled under the cardboard tables of Muslim vendors.

"I tried to connect with uncles living here only to discover the sad truth of their lives. Orphans and other stories you never heard about back in Ireland. One uncle wound up as a checker at a supermarket.

"But at one point, as I was sweating and wondering about getting a green card, I went to Ellis Island on me own. I got goose bumps. I was totally touched and moved by these people who had dreams and hopes and packed their bags and said their goodbyes and arrived here."

He soon discovered America's excesses, everything "beyond human size" diminishing him and making him unable to resolve his different aspects. He taught religious studies at a Catholic high school for girls; at the time, they had no problem with his homosexuality, he said, gazing into the black hole of his coffee for a moment. After receiving his green card he marched with the Irish Lesbians and Gay Organization in the St. Patrick's Day parade. Three weeks later, the Catholic school fired him for "unsatisfactory pedagogical skills," despite student protests. He sued the school for discrimination and eventually won a settlement, but having lost a job he loved, he was forced back into menial labor, first as a clerk at a lamp shop, then as a loader at a factory, and now—amused by the modern spin he was putting on a time-honored Irish occupation—a "chambermaid" at a Village guesthouse.

Even with his struggles here, more than any other immigrant I'd met, Brian *knew* why he was here—and it had nothing to do with the weather. He wasn't searching for a better wage or smarter restaurants. He was searching for personal freedom.

It had grown dark. We left the cafe and strolled the chilly sidewalks of the Village for a while. Brian showed me his favorite windows—antique lamps, elaborate flower wreaths, and overfed cats. "Next time, I'll tell you about when I was stabbed," he said, before disappearing down a dimly lit street of bare trees and delivery bikes.

———

The subway ride from my neighborhood to the north end of the Bronx was a long, tedious journey marked by gradually rotating demographics between exits and entryways. At one stop I noticed someone had risked standing on the electrified third rail to spray-paint "Shakespeare" on the wall.

I got off at the end of the line and started walking the edge of an enormous cemetery toward one of New York's most Irish-saturated neighborhoods, a tiny, endogenous place on the verge of decline and, as I was about to learn, as receptive to outsiders as to a viral attack.

A warm, steamy rain was falling, and autumn hung over the cemetery, this Gordian worm of little roads, larger-than-life mourning angels, crows, and the smell of vintage candle wax drifting up into ancient tree branches. On a map the roads of this cemetery had a distinctly Celtic design, and as I continued along a ragged footpath, I thought of Strabo, the ancient Greek geographer, who believed the Irish considered it an honor to devour their dead fathers.

Fleets of cars periodically swooshed by, spraying mud, but by the time I reached the neighborhood's main street, the sun had burned an eerie whiteness through the rain and down on the street's Irish bakeries, restaurants, and pubs, its storefronts awash in faded pastels and a familiar Irish bare-bonedness. There was something a bit Old West about the breadth of this street and its storefronts, lying low against a suburban sky. I stopped at a bakery cafe and ordered some tea. Every other table in the place was occupied by Irish couples or families, many of whom had remote, gaunt faces and clothes that seemed a decade out of fashion. They spoke quietly or not at all, with their heads down over their plates, and the woman sitting at the next table said everything three times. I read the news of Tipperary, which involved broken windows and stolen wallets. Before leaving I asked a waitress if there was a movie theater in the neighborhood, but she just blinked at me a couple times and asked, "Why?"

I crossed the street and found the immigration center, which looked like a back-street tax office. A poster on the wall described the "Properly Rolled Fingerprint," and the "Not" in a "Thank You for Not Smoking" sign had been gouged out. The office manager was a young man with long blond hair and a mustache. He explained that he was always careful to get out of this neighborhood before sundown be-cause of a gang of young Irish-American "yobs" or "narrow-backs." "Narrowback" was a slur used in New York slums of the late 1800s against Anglo-Saxons, an indication that the new Irish did not embrace Irish-Americans as their own. The "narrowback" gangs played a game up here called "donkey-bashing," in which they put native Irish into hos-pitals and sometimes the ground.

"Everyone knows who they are. You'll see them up the street here when you leave," the manager said, as if pointing out a tourist attraction. He seemed nervous. A few minutes passed; then a mother and daughter came in to ask him advice about getting back into the States without a green card. He leaned back in his chair, rattling a pen between his teeth. "Here's what you do . . ." He reeled off a few Borgian tips: equip the suitcase for a holiday in Florida—summer clothes and suntan lotion; don't pack any American products like Procter & Gamble deodorants or Kmart sweaters; expunge all American names from datebooks; and try to fly via London.

The 1924 immigration quota imposed by the United States had rarely been filled by the Irish until the late 1970s. In the 1980s, with an increase of immigrants the United States began restricting Irish entry, fostering a large amount of Irish "tourists" who came and never left, vanishing into the underworld of illegality. But for some, the illegality of life here was what drew them in the first place: it meant a larger, untaxed income.

After the mother and daughter left, I asked the office manager if he knew anyone around here who would talk to me. He thought for a moment and finally said no. "It's different up here."

After leaving the immigration center, I saw the gang where he said they'd be—teenagers in expensive high-tops, low-slung jeans, T-shirts, and baseball caps turned gangsta style. I'd heard a few theories about donkey-bashing, one being that thieves preyed on the Irish because, if here illegally, they'd never go to the police. Another theory involved a clash of the old Ireland with the new, more liberal Ireland. As one young woman had put it: "They think we're deviants or something, not upholding the old lace-curtain traditions. The Irish who came here in the 1950s can't accept that anything has changed back in Ireland." But no doubt "drink" also lay at the root of the violence.

It was a touchy subject. The native Irish drank for reasons that persisted—however remotely or subconsciously—from famine days, when whiskey distillation was not only an easy source of cash but a "remedy" for hunger and depression. Drinking came to be seen as an act of social cohesion and defiance. Irish-Americans, on the other hand, drank because they were "Irish," and like other transatlantic traditions, this one had warped a little in the crossing and became a tenacious, almost pathological self-stereotype.

I walked back to the subway feeling a little disheartened. New York's densest population of Irish had turned out to be its least inviting. But, at least here, it was understandable. Many of these immigrants were unskilled and illegal; they had good reason to avoid exposure. Previous migrant cultures in New York had also had this siege mentality, but there had been at least an internal loyalty there. After circling the wagons up here, it seemed the Irish had discovered the enemy was already inside and apparently I was one of those enemies.

When the rain turned suddenly torrential I stopped at a bar, populated that late Friday afternoon by an assortment of deadbeats, nihilists, and the marginally employed, all staring up at a television. The bartender was a Galway native; a peroxide blonde in a pink sweat suit, she strolled up and down the bar with a cigarette bobbing off the corner of her mouth. I sat at the end near the door to watch the rain and flip through a tabloid newspaper. The man next to me—

an American—was covered with Vietnam and shamrock
tattoos.

"If I won the lottery," the bartender said to him, "I'd go
mad in the head." She poured herself a shot of whiskey. At
one point the vet told me he only drank here because of
the cemetery across the street. "When I die all they'll have
to do is throw me over that wall and that'll be that." When
I eventually asked him and the bartender what they thought
of the Irish situation up here, a retired detective—a small,
steely Irish-American with a sour carnival barker's face—
jumped in.

"You're a writer or something, aren't you, kid?" He asked
me. "I can tell by the way your fingernails are cut. And you
been askin' a lot of dumb questions." He leaned over and
pointed his cigarette at me. "Look, kid, if you go around
here asking questions about donkey-bashing and all that,
they're going to send you home in a body bag." He grimaced
as if he'd just tasted something tart. "After everything that's
happened here?"

By then, it had gotten dark, the rain was still lashing
down. The bartender called me a cab.

"Watch yourself, kid," the detective said, before turning
back to his beer as if it presented a long night's work.

The cabby looked as if he'd just stepped out of some
grainy 1970s documentary about death row, but I climbed
into the front seat next to him.

"Wet night," he said. His voice was hoarse from years of
smoke and he had a Northern Ireland accent, so that "wet
night" sounded like "wade nide." His name was Hugh
Brolly, and, as it turned out, for some he *was* dangerous. But

he was soft-spoken, and as far as I was concerned, he had an optimistic candor I appreciated at that moment.

"First time I came here," he told me, "my visa ran out, so I went ahead and changed the numbers on it. Well, you can't do that. That shows you how naive I was. I used to live in Texas but I was in duress and came here to find my people."

The car radio crackled and two voices bantered back and forth.

> Driver: I got a search party here. The guy is lost trying to find this church.
> Dispatcher: Do you have the name of this church?
> Driver: No name. No street.
> Dispatcher: How can you get there if you don't know where you're going?

Hugh smiled at this, and laugh lines crimped around his shark-gray eyes.

"I enjoy driving a cab, meeting people and getting them home safe. I've never been robbed. I do good when trouble comes my way, though. I start out diplomatically, see, not aggressively, although sometimes you have to use force with some people to get them to understand what you're saying. I picked up a black woman one night and took her to a rough area, this big stone building among all these apartment buildings that looked like rockets. I helped her with her bags and she said to me, 'Now, son, you know this is not the right area for you to be in.' I said, 'Okay, ma'am.' Then she showed me how to get out of there, because she said if you get caught the boys here will take you out." He put one hand on his chest. "She had that mother instinct toward me."

We passed a group of young African-Americans on a corner.

"There are some fine young Irish boys now," Hugh joked. We rode in silence for a few miles before he added, "Where I'm from, they were doing the same to us as they done to the blacks in South Africa."

He explained that he came from a family of nine children and three bedrooms in a public housing estate in a Catholic industrial working-class area in Derry called Bogside, where most of the women worked in textile factories and 80 percent of the men stayed home to raise children and race greyhounds.

"I can remember a normal time," he said, referring to the days before "the Troubles," when the Bogside estate entrance had been closed down against British forces by the IRA. In no time Hugh's interests shifted from cricket to carjacking.

"Teachers figured I was a lost cause," he said. " 'Hugh,' they said to me, 'the way you're going now you'll end up dead.' But the only time I was really scared was on Bloody Sunday when British troops killed thirteen peaceful marchers. I thought they were going to kill us all."

Using a *Man from U.N.C.L.E.* spy kit, a Christian Brother helped Hugh forge his baptismal records so it would appear that he was old enough to join the Irish Army.

"I felt safer in the Army," he said without irony. During his stint most of his friends ended up in prison and one died on a hunger strike, so when Hugh returned to Derry he felt obliged to take up where they'd left off.

"I done an operation," he said rather casually, "and ended up going to prison for kidnapping and armed robbery."

I was going to ask him about this, but by then we had reached my subway stop at Fourteenth Street. Hugh put the cab in neutral, then turned up the radio and began singing along to Paul Simon's "Mother and Child Reunion."

"What a coincidence," he said, and turned toward me, as excited as a child. "My mother is coming to visit in a few weeks."

———

When she was thirteen, my mother ran away from home and, because of Sarah's inaction, stayed away for months. By all accounts, Sarah had been a rigid woman who did not distribute affection among her six daughters with an even hand. In turn, her daughters felt they never really understood her. When Sarah returned to Roscrea, after much ongoing persuasion from her daughters, some of them accompanied her and for the first time were able to see Sarah in the context of her family and her past, which was enlightening. As my Aunt Ceil put it: "We finally realized, oh, she's *Irish*." Apparently, just before deciding to make the trip, Sarah's sister Chris—the one who'd also gone to New York but didn't stay long—was close to death and told one of her daughters, "I would die happy if I could see Sarah one more time." News of Sarah's arrival came just days later; Chris made a miraculous recovery, jumped out of bed, and arranged to have the walls of her house repapered, then, during Sarah's visit, did all the cooking. The first thing

Sarah told everyone when she stepped through Chris's doorway was "My daughters never touch alcohol," which was, as she knew, not strictly true. She held a sometimes mischievous matriarchal hold over them, but, ultimately, she was a proud, protective mother who could be relied on during hard times, and in the end, she earned her daughters' respect.

Chris died not long after Sarah's visit. Ten years later, at the age of ninety-four, Sarah had a stroke and lay in a hospital, where I spent one night with her, sitting in a chair. That was the last time I saw her; but I realized that she died with considerably more than the five dollars she arrived with. In trying to determine her motives for leaving Ireland, I remembered one thing she told me not long before she died. Her maiden name used to be O'Reilly, but somewhere along the way it became Reilly. With one amnesiac blow she lost any symbolic connection to a people and a place. But this is what we do—bury ancestral offenses as unconsciously as animals. The "O" was not important, she told me, and I needn't bother myself with it.

But many Irish had since told me the "O" was important or should be. In fact, some people I'd spoken to here saw the elimination of the "O" as an act of hostility toward the old country.

NOVEMBER

The days were growing shorter. A friend and I ate cold borscht in a midtown diner and discussed the planetary influences on his life. Trees in the park turned bright red, and globe lamps flickered on a little earlier each day as the lights of rush-hour traffic flashed through the trees in long, reassuring streams.

One morning I took the subway to Manhattan, where summer still lingered between the stone and steel blocks. I was to meet Ann Hamilton, a modest, unaffected woman with long strawberry-blond hair, intensely green eyes, and a pretty, rather somber face.

Every three or four years Ann's family had moved from one lighthouse to another along the coast of Ireland, living in the most isolated peninsular land stations in the country in what was a long family tradition of protecting voyagers from Ireland's deadly outcrops.

"It was very uprooting," she'd told me in an earlier conversation. Sometimes, in coastal towns, her father lived separately from the family on the lighthouse island, and it would seem at times as if they had a beam of light instead of a father. "At one point, we lived in the North and could see Scotland on a clear day, but up there if you come from Cork you might as well come from France. Family migration in Ireland is almost unheard of. They are either planted or leave the country altogether. For me too, the thought of going to Dublin to study was horrifying even though it was only a couple hours away. New York seemed closer."

The family eventually lived permanently in Sligo Town, where Ann studied business at a regional college. She left Ireland ten years ago and was now a dress designer living in a renovated warehouse along the Hudson River.

My subway ride was brief. A young Chinese man next to me furiously scribbled in his journal. Out on the street a breeze that seemed to originate from some distant apple orchard cut through the Indian summer heat.

Ann's apartment had an understated funkiness—like a page from the Sears, Roebuck catalogue dipped in desert colors—with racks of dresses and hats and a sewing dummy leaning against a wall.

She'd been in bed for the past week with back pain and wasn't sure if she was feeling any better, but she suggested we go eat lunch somewhere. "I've got to get out of here," she said. We headed for a French diner in the nearby meatpacking district, Ann walking with pain-induced dignity. "I'm a little spacey with these Doan's pills," she warned me. As we crossed a street, we caught a glimpse of New Jersey, this smear of color through the car exhaust hanging over the highway.

"My great-uncle lives over there somewhere," she said, "but he had a very tough time here and . . . we're not in touch."

We reached the streets of the meatpacking district, where the brick cross streets were encrusted with sawdust and bluebottle flies. Fortunately, the diner, which was ensconced amid all this carnivorous gloom, had a sleek, chilled atmosphere with clean cheerful chrome-and-maroon chairs.

We sat down next to a table full of agents passing a cellular phone back and forth.

"I hate those phones," Ann whispered.

I asked her how her early impressions of American life contrasted with its reality.

"I remember seeing *The Brady Bunch* as a kid. I thought it was unusual that two families could get together like that.

Of course," she added wistfully—and rather seriously—
"Carol's husband died and Mike's wife died, but they seemed
so lighthearted."

She paused to butter a piece of toast. "You know, I never
wanted to emigrate. I never had that much courage and
wasn't greatly adventurous. But I was feeling stuck there in
the early 1980s and everyone was emigrating and it seemed
that everything was getting worse. And I hated New York.
I didn't like the air, the lack of community, the isolation
between cultures."

After she worked as a nanny, while taking night classes
at the Parsons School of Design for four years, she got her
green card and her first "real" job designing moderate-priced
clothes for department stores. Now she worked for herself.

After lunch, we walked back along a quiet avenue, then
stopped at a corner to talk some more before parting ways.

"I used to feel alienated whenever I went back to visit
Ireland," she told me. "I was afraid that I might sound
American or speak too openly. The Irish, as you know, don't
always say what they're thinking."

————

I got off on the wrong subway stop one day on my way to
meet an Irish priest and found myself in the middle of one
of Brooklyn's "bad" neighborhoods: empty buildings, store-
front churches, rubble lots, pawnshops, and young boys staring into beepers. A teddy bear lay on top of a pile of roof
shingles. But as I walked, the streets grew friendlier. Old
men in straw hats played cards on the sidewalk, and young
girls in bright skirts breezed in and out of shops. When I
finally reached Father Kelly's cramped office and took a seat

in front of his desk, he read his mail out loud to me. "I live on the slopes of Mount Kenya," he boomed, as his large black eyeglasses slipped down his nose. He frowned, then tossed the letter aside, picking up another to riffle through it. "Let's see if we get any money in this one," he said to me. He was a fleshy, rather exasperated man with wispy hair and a blunt manner, a man who changed people's lives with applications and documents rather than idealism. He occasionally broke into song: "Oh, sweet Adare, Oh, lovely vale . . ."

Father Kelly had trained with the Christian Brothers, attended St. John's in Waterford and a seminary in Rome before coming directly here to St. Brigid's Church in Bushwick, putting himself in the unique position of witnessing the downfall and uncertain recovery of a Brooklyn neighborhood rather than fleeing it as so many Irish had.

After the Depression, this area's mostly German population was replaced by Italians, then African-Americans and Puerto Ricans. As the drug economy slipped in, many moved out; the area lost city services; factories closed down; and the big blackout of 1977 further crippled it with rampant arson and looting. You could say it was one of those neighborhoods on which the 1970s descended like a forge blast.

"My own father wasn't particularly pleased that I left home. He gets great ribbing at the fact that he has a son in America and yet gets no money from him."

Father Kelly was now both the church curate and a lawyer, specializing in immigration law, helping mostly Puerto Ricans, El Salvadorans, Dominicans, Mexicans, and the occasional Irish.

"The church is a great haven for immigrants. It defends them and they find power in numbers. Most of New York's churches are filled with immigrants. I'm the only Irishman left in this neighborhood. I believe there's still one German lady living here. She's ancient. Whenever she sees me she says, 'I'm still here,' " he called out, waving a meaty hand and grinning in imitation of her. A few years ago Father James was jumped by drug dealers who mistakenly believed he was letting police use the church bell tower for surveillance.

"These days I never wear my collar. Being a priest in New York City, my dear, they look at you like you're queer, you're a child molester, there's something wrong with you. I do remember a time when cripples and priests could get into Radio City Music Hall for free." He gave me a prolonged, asthmatic smile to see if I caught the irony.

When I asked him about the new wave of Irish, he leaned over his desk and began flipping through his mail again while he spoke, occasionally pausing to read in silence, one finger in the air.

"Most of the Irish who come are not the poor, as they were once upon a time. Most are leaving good jobs behind and coming here for the adventure and for more money. What's interesting is that some of them accept the sexual mores but not so much the social policies. They considered themselves liberals in Ireland, but when they got here and mingled with other ethnic groups they turned into rednecks." He tossed a few items of mail into the garbage, disgusted not by the mail but by the dubious evolution of these younger immigrants. "They get their high-paying jobs, then turn around and demand a more stringent immigration policy, and the more money they make, the more intolerant they are of others."

As he spoke, I remembered the one thing that Father Kelly had that other immigrants did not—a vow of stability.

—·—

I received a letter today from my cousin Maureen O'Connor in Roscrea. She wrote:

"You will be sorry to hear John died. R.I.P. . . . Now that he is gone I feel lost."

DECEMBER

It was an exceptional Greenwich Village dusk: a scotch-colored sunset brushed the tops of trees and town houses; Christmas lights sparkled like sea ice in the subzero temperatures; and the distant Empire State Building stood awash in blue light to mark Frank Sinatra's birthday. Brian Doyle was telling me about the time he'd been stabbed. He was pulling sheets out of a dryer when I arrived at the guesthouse where he worked as its chambermaid. It was a historic building of narrow hallways, garden rooms, Balinese art, and obsolete wall maps. A fire blazed in the hearth of its double parlor as he and I folded sheets together.

"You could say I'd been New Yorked. It was an August night. I had just finished work and was getting off the subway at about eleven o'clock at night." He dropped one corner of the sheet momentarily to reach around and touch his back. "Out of the blue I felt a huge thump here. It was a blunt sensation in my back, not a sharp one like you'd think. I saw this guy on a bike and I remember he called me a faggot. I went into a daze, thinking: Jesus, there'll be an awful lot of people organizing céilís." (A ceílí was a social gathering in which money was raised to help Irish who'd fallen on sudden hard times.)

The stabbing happened three years ago; the attacker had been arrested and imprisoned, but Brian still spoke of it with disbelief and an appalled smile. "I staggered up the street shouting for help." The knife had punctured his lung. During the week he spent recovering in Bellevue, police officially classified the attack a bias crime and suddenly Brendan's name became part of a rallying cry against the Catholic Church by gay activists, producing T-shirts with "Brian Doyle has a knife in his back."

"I hated all that political stuff," he said. "The mayor stood by my hospital bed and made a speech. But in retrospect I don't think it was a bias crime." He paused to divulge the trade secrets of folding form-fitted sheets, then leaned against the dryer, his mind apparently racing with New York's many forces of corruption, from its dust to its knives. After a moment he sighed and pulled some towels out of the dryer with renewed resolve.

"A year later I was interrogated for three hours by detectives in Brooklyn who accused me of being a drug dealer and of being involved in this big cover-up. That was more terrifying than the stabbing itself." He handed me some pillowcases and added with a wry grin, "New York's finest."

After folding the laundry Brian scrubbed the parlor floor on his hands and knees, the Pine-Sol odors mixing with the slightly oily smell of the fireplace. As he crawled under the parlor's baby grand piano, he talked over his shoulder about his current circumstances, the waste of his education, frustrated ambitions to teach, and how his struggle for personal expression had literally brought him to his knees. "It's funny," he said, sitting back on his haunches. "The historical Irish group that I now have the most understanding of or feeling for are those young Irish maids and servant girls." He wrung water out of the sponge—"as you can imagine"—and went back to work.

—⁓—

On certain afternoons the winter light hit New York low and hard. I'd tape tinfoil on the windows to keep it out. On the weekends my husband and I took walks through the park in long, heavy coats. We spent the afternoons in bookstores and pool halls or rode the elevated train into the city. When it ran aboveground the train gave us a view of Manhattan's cold, reflecting skyline.

Rosie Kiernan understood some of the more transcendental aspects of the city. One day she told me about her first day waitressing in Manhattan at a restaurant located near the Empire State Building. "Have you ever looked up at the Empire State Building when you're right underneath it?" she asked me in exasperation. "You can't see it. I actually stopped by a church and prayed to find it, but the thing is, Joan, you can be standing right under it and you don't realize you're there."

We were sitting in the Scratcher at a wooden table with a votive candle burning between us. A short-haired sheepdog kept trotting back and forth between tables to be scratched behind the ears.

"Mother didn't want me to come here at all," she said. "Her cousin was murdered here in 1972."

Rosie, who now worked as a nanny, was an earthy, blunt, and energetic woman with long brown hair and a face that might have seemed sour and unattainable were it not for her warmth and irrepressible good humor.

"If I'd known what my first six months in New York would be like I'd have never come." She arrived originally with the assurance from an older uncle that he'd help her get a green card. So she and two friends moved to his place in a remote peninsular section of Queens. Her uncle turned out to be a "strange character, an Irishman from way back," who was employed by the government in some mysterious capacity—she never knew how—going off to work wearing various disguises. When she arrived, not only did he refuse to help her get a green card but he did everything he could to keep her prisoner in his house.

"He didn't want us working because we were illegal. He wouldn't let us get an apartment," she said, reckoning his sins on her fingers. "He wouldn't take our money for anything, but then he'd throw his generosity in our faces. And worst of all, he told me the Kiernan family back in Ireland meant nothing to him."

After six months of his misguided hospitality she and her friends found an apartment in Queens, and Rosie began waitressing near the Empire State Building, using her Ireland home phone number as a false social security number. She resented being illegal because her grandmother had worked here at the turn of the century. At one point, Rosie went home for her brother's wedding and had trouble getting back through Kennedy. "I said to your man, 'If you let me through here, I'll behave meself.' But he gave me an awful riddling and sent me to be interrogated, but the interrogator, an

Irish-American, thank God, just said, 'Have a nice holiday, goodbye.' " After that she didn't dare return to her family's Longford farm again for another four years.

Rosie now lived in Woodside, Queens, and, typical of the Irish who gravitated to this particular neighborhood, she came to the States for the "good time" rather than for economic reasons and for Irish rather than American culture. I thought of the phrase she used earlier concerning the Empire State Building—you don't realize you're there—and how it seemed to be the axiom of Rosie's ten years in New York. "Someone asked me about living in New York once," she said, "and I had to actually stop and ask myself, 'Am I living in New York?' "

In a few months Rosie planned to go back to Ireland and marry a Mayo businessman.

"God willing," she added caustically. "If I don't kill him first."

I realized Rosie, like Tom Weir, was about to move back to Ireland, and maybe it was this prospect that gave them a kind of genial distance from their immigrant experience. A chapter in their lives had ended. Tom felt anchored in two countries; Rosie chose Ireland, having never left it in her mind.

The sheepdog, who'd made the circuit around the bar, had returned and was leaning hard against Rosie's leg. "It's going to be hard to be dependent on somebody," she told the dog, then looked back at me. "I've been independent so long. But I know in me heart I'm doing the right thing. It'll be strange to be back. No Chinese food at eleven o'clock at night. No four o'clock bar-closing times. But Irish after-hours are brilliant . . . the forbidden fruit."

Rosie also shared the new fatalism of young Irish immigrants, illegals especially, leading such precarious lives, returning home with stories, not of adventure and fortune, but of rats, muggings, and misunderstandings, coloring American streets something much darker than the gold that once paved them.

"An amazing creature, the roach," Rosie said. "They crunch when you kill them. I brought some rubber ones home to Ireland for everyone to see."

JANUARY

Hugh Brolly and I sat in his cab, which he drove all night until dawn. It had a busted cylinder and shook violently at low speeds as we drove aimlessly around the Bronx through areas that were alternately urban—car alarms, hospital sprawl—and suburban—crickets, a raccoon lumbering on spindly legs through the twilight. Most of his passengers were young Irishmen, and Hugh either chatted with them about the weather or music or, if he trusted them, continued to relate the details of his life to me. When we picked up a scowling old Irish-American in a baseball cap, Hugh winked at me, indicating that he didn't want to talk in front of this particular fare.

"Weather good," Hugh suggested, looking at the man in the rearview mirror. The man grunted, then after an indecisive pause said, "Winter." Hugh asked the man what he did for a living.

"I drive a school bus now," the man said, guardedly.

"You must enjoy that with the childer," Hugh suggested.

"Long damn day is what it is."

We dropped the old man off and picked up another fare, a skinny young woman with a tubercular cough: "It's the car that's shaking? I thought I had a nervous condition."

Hugh resumed his story about the kidnapping and armed robbery job.

"We were captured by the British. They raided my mother's house the day I was arrested, but she faked a heart attack to keep them from tearing her house apart. Myself, I was sentenced to eight years but only spent four in Long Kesh prison camp. When the screw came in every morning to count us, I always heard that door being unlocked and that sound was a reminder every day that I was in a place that wasn't a nice place to be. After my release my mother said, 'You get away out of here,' and my father said, 'Don't stay in this country, son, go.' It was for me to do the journey. All I had to do was open the right doors and I was very happy, so I was."

He went to the Gulf coast of Texas, where a sister lived.

"The cowgirls were fascinated with me," he said, shocked by his luck. He worked on construction sites, married a waitress, drove a Cordoba, divorced, married again and fathered a son. "It was important to me to plant roots in this here country." But he had now been divorced for a year.

"What happened was, I lost my temper and dislocated my wife's finger when I pushed her. Everything started going down the drain. I was so disheartened I left there last year and came to New York to sort myself out. Irish immigrants help each other. I wouldn't be here if only for them."

At that point we turned onto a dark isolated street where a car had just been set on fire; as we passed, the flames shot up into tree branches and a wave of scorching heat briefly penetrated the cab interior. When we were a few hundred feet beyond it, the car exploded behind us, sending glass in all directions, the conflagration dancing like small fireballs in the cab's rearview mirrors.

A few minutes later the dispatcher called in to tell Hugh someone had requested to be picked up by him.

"Who is it?"

"The pope."

We stopped at the address, which was a bar. A lean man with an unnerved look in his eyes and a sheepish grin climbed in the back seat.

"This here's Tony," Hugh told me. "We grew up to-gether." Back in Derry, Hugh informed me, Tony had been known for his ingenious designs of homemade guns, but he now designed his own guitars.

"Tony, what do you remember of Bloody Sunday?" Hugh asked him, looking at his rearview mirror.

Tony scooched forward and put his arms across the back of the seat. "There were bullets everywhere," he said. "My da, he knew I'd seen people killed, so that night he took me across the border to see the ocean. 'Look at the water, son,' he said to me."

"It's all right, Tony," Hugh said.

"I always try to forget."

"How could you forget? You couldn't."

Hugh told me about his mother: how a soldier broke her nose; how troops fired rubber bullets into her ankles; and how her house had been raided nineteen times. During raids soldiers tore up linen baskets, drawers, cut shirts open, and put plastic bags over everyone's hands to catch evidence of nitroglycerine, although it was a substance that could rub off something as innocuous as a deck of cards. The women on his street used to gather stones in their skirts to throw at troops; they soaked rags in vinegar and put them along the hedges for those who'd been gassed; they rattled garbage-can lids on the streets to let people know troops were coming, but of the sixty-two mothers living in their area at the time, Hugh said, there were only four left, the rest having died of heart attacks and other stress-related diseases.

"I have a question to ask you, Hughie," Tony said. "If God came here and says to you would you live it over, would you?"

"I wouldn't change it."

"I wouldn't either."

"What happened in Derry just opened the door," Hugh told me, "and thousands of us rushed through, some with their talent, some with the sadness that we had."

We drove in silence for a while; when our cab pulled up alongside another cab to wait at a light, Tony stuck his head out the window. "Do you have any Grey Poupon?"

At midnight we stopped at a bar and went inside for club soda. In the 1980s this area, and in particular Bain-bridge Avenue, was notorious for partying, but it had since deteriorated into a tragicomic picture of decadence. Some-one once told me that after a night in the bars up here you'd want to burn your clothes. Hugh called it "God's country."

"To be here in America gives you a sense of something," he said, leaning over the bar. "A sense of yourself." He added that here he'd been treated like an Irishman rather than a Catholic minority, which was, in itself, quite liber-ating. "But one thing I don't like about here is that when trouble comes down on you in Ireland you can always get another dream, but in America there is just the one dream. It's like Lady Liberty reaches out to you with one hand, then slaps you with the other."

Before we parted Hugh told me one more thing about his release from prison.

"I took a brick and threw it back at the gate. We all done this, reason being if you throw a rock back at a place as you leave it, you'll never have to go back there again."

—⁓—

Not long after that night with Hugh—just as I was wondering how much of an anomaly he was—he disappeared. I called his home number; it had been disconnected. I called his cab company; the dispatcher had no idea where he'd gone.

—⁓—

Rosie and I were sitting in the kitchen of an Upper East Side apartment where she'd worked as a nanny for the last year, located in a red brick building with cracked frosted windows and wheezing radiators.

"A nanny is a goat," she corrected me. "I mind other people's children, bash them around a bit, and put manners on them."

Michael, her three-year-old charge, was standing at the kitchen door with a bright dimpled face and oversized red sweater and jeans.

"You drive me to do what, Michael?" she asked him.

He hung his head and put his arms behind his back, hiding a smile. "I drive you to drink, Rosie."

"Look at the face on you, you cheeky monkey," she said,

handing him a Fig Newton. He took the cookie and with mock solemnity marched into the next room. Rosie turned and started rifling through kitchen drawers in search of a chocolate biscuit. "I won't drink my tea without one." After settling on a Fig Newton she sat on a counter stool and leaned her head against the wall. She was clearly tired, but she also had great reserves of energy, and as her workday was coming to a close a certain fervor had begun to creep into her eyes.

"I worked with one family for five years and leaving them was the hardest thing I ever had to do. I grew to love the children as my own. The family I work with now is great. My mother asked me what nationality they were. I told her the mother is American Catholic and the father is Jewish. She said she supposed a Catholic Jew was all right."

We walked into the living room to watch Michael play with a phonics machine. "Lord," Rosie said, after we plopped down on the floor, "when I think of the horror stories of other girls, forced to cook and clean, working long hours for shit wages, then having their passports taken off them and literally held prisoner. Worse, I heard of a Philippine girl. The child she watched was hit in the head with a swing and died a few days later." We talked some more about what it was like to be a nanny and how it was more socially desirable to be a nanny here than to work back in a factory in Ireland.

When Michael's mother arrived home, she told me how "devastated" they were that Rosie was leaving and that they wanted to find another Irish girl to make the transition easier on Michael. As Rosie and I prepared to leave, Michael tried to persuade Rosie to stay by offering to read to her.

"He's a heartbreaker, that one," Rosie said as we walked down through the building's high-pitched echoes.

On the street we hailed a cab and headed toward her Queens neighborhood, crossing the river as a peach light trimmed the tops of buildings over an otherwise flat gray landscape of old billboards for staples and girdles.

"I keep looking at everything thinking it'll be the last time I'll see it," Rosie said.

We got out of the cab at a main thoroughfare, a clean bustling strip of specialty shops and diners—one Irish bar featuring sumo wrestling—under the shadow of an elevated train, which was called the "immigrant train" because this area was considered a first stop for Irish along with a variety of Hispanic and Asian cultures. Rosie seemed to think the area was "going downhill" and cited a newly opened nude bar as advance notice of urban blight. She shared an apartment with another Irish girl, a transitory place full of knick-knacks, unpacked boxes, an exercise machine, and a kitchen table blanketed with junk mail.

We stopped for dinner at an Indian restaurant, where the proprietor gave Rosie a hug. "It's been a long time."

"Have you missed my bullshit?" she asked him. He handed us menus.

"Are you married?" she asked him.

"Yes."

"Oh dear," she said, expressing sympathy. Weddings and their inherent fiascoes was a subject she would return to all night.

"I took strips off my fiancé last night," she told me. "I mailed all the invitations going to England, Germany, and

Spain, and he only had to send the Irish ones, which he hadn't done yet. I told him I'm marrying a thoroughbred eejit."

After dinner we went to an Irish bar with old railroad motifs. The bartender was a watery-eyed young man with a long nose and an ever-narrowing face that gave him the look of some lesser Dick Tracy villain. As he wiped the bar, he and Rosie talked about horse racing and golf; at one point she teased him about one of his ex-girlfriends.

"She's always stirring the auld muck," he told me out of the corner of his mouth, pointing a thumb at Rosie.

"You poor eejit, you," Rosie told him—frequently.

After finishing a beer we went to another Irish bar down the street, where Rosie and the bartender discussed various popular reception halls in Ireland.

At one point a young man entered the bar, loaded down with several bags and a mixed expression of confusion, excitement, and fear. He nodded uncertainly at the bartender. Everyone at the bar glanced at him, immediately pegging him for a greenhorn. The bartender gave him an exaggerated up-and-down glance of appraisal, then offered his hand. "How are ye?" The young man grabbed his hand as if it were a life preserver, a look of relief washing over his face. He ordered a pint. "Just in, are you?" the bartender asked.

Rosie watched this interchange. All night long she'd been looking at everything as if seeing it for the last time, but the moment the greenhorn walked into the bar she began seeing everything through his eyes, again as if for the first time.

"Poor kid. I feel so bad for him."

I talked to the Irish until certain eye-opening conclusions began to develop and would not go away. Many returned to Ireland; some came back again. There was a segment who had children and settled down in the suburbs. This was, in part, a response to the flood of non-Irish immigrants to the city, the unprecedented numbers of unskilled Third World populations, which had sparked considerable controversy. There were those who said this new trend of immigration would burden and ultimately ruin the country, while others rebuked this idea as racist. Like the Irish, this new wave of immigrants had a growing sense that America wasn't so much the land of freedom as the land of free enterprise. But I believed America's immigrants reflected America itself—the two were inextricable. If more immigrants came to exploit our system, then they were reflecting our own exploitative society. If they failed to assimilate in our multiculturally friendly society, then they were reflecting what had become an already deeply fissured society. For years we'd been sending out radar across the world's time zones, and we were now hearing the return signal.

Amid this inrush each group existed in its own strange little vacuum, but within these, and within the Irish one in particular, I detected an interesting alchemy. As their self-doubts, disappointment, and fear pushed the Irish together, they were discovering an Ireland they would never have found in Ireland itself. People from Dublin talked to those from Galway, the Irish of the North talked to those of the South; it was possible Ireland could find unity only away from its own borders. The Irish came to discover America, only to discover themselves, and they didn't always like what they saw.

Brona Crehan read some of my interviews with her fellow immigrants. "They made me . . . uncomfortable," she said. "You know, embarrassed."

One day, while transcribing a taped conversation I discovered that two different voices from two sides of the tape had bled together, making the entire tape garbled and untranscribable. This was the treacherously personal side of technology. Thermosensitivity, ferric formulations, and digital coding had brought people together, then created new ways to keep them apart, and it seemed that in the past few months especially—perhaps by seeing it through Irish immigrants—I had become more aware of how technology had prompted a heightened, if not deluded, concern for "public image," and how, in general, it was fashioning a world no longer of place but of process.

But a surreal kind of sense began to emerge from the voices; a sentence begun by one voice was occasionally finished by the other.

"Irish have contributed to America's success" . . . "The Irish are dispensable."

"It's a drinking culture" . . . "of tea and water."

It was as if two worlds were struggling out of that nonsense, like the two images of Ireland clashing in the collective Irish-American mind. But a third Ireland had been conjured by technology over the past 150 years, an Oz or Atlantis of shamrocks and lace curtains born amid barnacles and plankton ooze about the time the first transatlantic telegraph cable was being laid across the ocean floor.

Today Ireland had one of Europe's most modern digital

telecommunication systems. Manufacturing fueled its economy—Europe's fastest-growing. Companies were actively recruiting from abroad, encouraging emigrants to come home, and all those doing so were, in turn, transforming an entrenched country into a more forward-thinking one. Ireland had become a viable place to live; it was growing into the imaginations that once outgrew it, and this cast doubts in the hearts of those living here in New York. I discovered through a mutual acquaintance that Michael Maguire and his wife returned to Ireland because she'd been offered a high-paying job, greatly reducing the odds of their son becoming President of the United States. Some avoided me, having been reluctant to tell a story that, as yet, had no ending; while others had been reluctant to see the story ended.

My grandmother was one of these. Her six years in New York had been an exciting but isolated phase in her life, and she didn't know that much about her husband before they married. When he was eight years old he emigrated with his parents from Canada to Michigan, where his father farmed his own land. At one point his parents bought a restaurant in order to send their daughters to college, leaving James and his brothers to farm. James was a politically active, "saintly" man who always took strangers in and fed them. Before deciding to venture out with him, Sarah wrote James's parish priest asking if the Mitchells were drunkards; the priest wrote back they were not, so she and James married and traveled west along with the other eight million immigrants to do so between 1892 and 1924.

Their journey ended in Clare County, Michigan, a place with familiar terrain named for Ireland's County Clare. They lived several miles outside a small town that had one Catholic church and a beer garden on every corner. A cousin of mine had recorded Sarah's memories of her first day there.

"The rain poured down on us as we waited for our ride. My blue cotton dress, once neatly pressed, and my blue wide-brimmed hat were wrinkled and wet from the train ride and weather. In both hands we carried all my belongings. I thought it was the last place God made, and He forgot to finish it. But I felt I was home for the first time since I left Ireland."

She must have stashed her latest fashions and hatboxes away, and although she continued to attend dances and inflame jealousy across the county, backbreaking work now superseded her formerly carefree existence.

With the help of land grants and loans from his parents James bought a piece of land a little larger than the base of the Empire State Building, and over the years the acreage accumulated to roughly the size of Chinatown.

Sarah felt more comfortable in towns and cities, having discovered America's more feral energies—its twisters and rising rivers. She didn't have the flexibility for farm life. She needed to control everything around her, and the weather constantly troubled her, even after she moved to town. During thunderstorms she lit candles and threw holy water on us. It wasn't until I had lived in New York for a while that I understood her fear of the deceiving calm that seems to rise from wells and root cellars. Whenever I board a west-bound train into the rural Midwest the notion of it tugs at me like the subterranean pull on a dowser's pendulum. Images of industrially orphaned corridors of land pass and fade under the loose ends and power lines of the kind of small towns that don't figure too largely on maps. What you do see on these maps, however, is how fear gradually replaced hope—place names like New York and New London seemed to evolve westward into saint's names and, with what must have been longing for other lands, Warsaw and Paris.

After James died, Sarah sold the farm and moved into town, where by then the churches outnumbered the beer gardens. At family reunions she would sit with an unreserved smile on her face, watching the numerous people she put on earth.

An estimated 75,000 Irish had become legal, permanent residents in New York City since 1988, and clearly the Irish presence on this side of the Atlantic would be felt for some time. But with every decade of the twentieth century, Irish immigration numbers had declined. On top of that, pressures back home were abating: people were having fewer children, and jobs were being created. There was still a 12 percent unemployment rate, however, and many unskilled would continue to leave the country, along with the perennial adventurers. But the signs were there.

"Who knows?" Father Kelly said of the future of Irish immigration. "It might well become a thing of the past."

I made plans to visit Roscrea for a couple of weeks, looking forward to the chance to knock on any door and be asked inside. When I dialed a Roscrea hotel an Irish directory operator asked me, "Roscrea? How odd. Are you sure you're going there?"

ROSCREA, COUNTY TIPPERARY

GIVEN THE recent talk of "huge" changes, when I arrived I began a list of them all: banks had been computerized; the movie theater was closed down; there were blueprints to turn the convent into a health club; and a new highway now crossed the edge of town, its overpass having been dubbed the Wailing Bridge because of the sound the wind made passing under its deck. A new shopping mall had been built at the center of town— a product of what some called "multinational poaching"— but it was hidden behind old storefronts, thus maintaining, at least on the face of it, Roscrea's ancient appearance.

But then one night I had drinks in my hotel pub with a couple who did not see Roscrea in terms of change. They'd lived for a year on Long Island, where Billie had worked in construction and Paula had been an au pair; both had lost weight because of the "plasticky" food and both had cheerfully lost money at the three-card monte tables in Times Square.

"I loved it," Billie said, touching Paula's arm in deference to her opposing opinion. He struck me as a man who longed to be at the center of things, leaning forward in his chair, his eyes dancing as if he could see the words you spoke. He had large weather-cracked hands and talked at an astonishingly rapid pace. "I would go back there tomorrow and never come back. If you work there you get paid. Here they won't pay you if they think they can get away with it."

He was a farmer now and would always be a farmer, because, as he put it, despite his diverse skills if he looked for work in Roscrea tomorrow he'd be lucky if they handed him a shovel.

Paula now worked at the ribbon factory. She was amiable, withdrawn, and in every way Billie's opposite. But one thing they learned from their experience, she said quietly, was that once you've emigrated, no matter how long you've been gone you're always an emigrant; people who hadn't been to America in ten years were still asked how long they'd been home for.

"And when you come back here," Billie added, "the world is at a standstill."

—⁓—

After three days I abandoned my list of changes and began observing the "standstill," with a certain amount of guilty satisfaction. It was cold and gold strips of light hung beneath banks of gray clouds the day I headed out to the fish farm.

"The wind would shave you," Thomas greeted me, shaking my hand. "How you keeping? You got taller." We talked about his mother, Chris, who'd died a month before.

"She had a great run," he said sadly. "Death takes an awful gap, Joan. It's part of you gone."

I had seen Chris's grave in the cemetery—where the older the dates, the younger the dead—still overflowing with fresh flowers.

I asked about his wife, who'd been expecting a baby the last time I was here; she'd since had that baby and another baby, the sixth, a couple of years later. "She's in great form," Thomas said. "The children are flying. They're great." We drank our tea in silence for a moment, then he nodded toward the pink walls. "That's a cold color."

———

One day Kathleen Beck and I took a walk around a boggy lake and discussed her upcoming trip to Asia. When we returned to her house Hugh came into the sitting room from the kitchen—where he'd been cooking dinner for us—and stared at me with his hands on his hips. "You're still at it?" he finally gasped. After dinner we sat in front of their large stone fireplace while Kathleen sewed the edges of a quilt she planned to send to Bosnia, and discussed various unresolvable topics like religion and crime. Hugh read some poetry to us, and occasionally broke into folk songs as they came to him.

"They'll be dragging rocks with that," he finally said to Kathleen in an effort to keep her from sending the quilt to Bosnia. "It will get blown up!"

———

One afternoon I visited Anthony Maher at the convent. "You can see the way I've been," he told me in the art room as he chopped tobacco in his palm. "Nothing has changed, although I did move further away from Roscrea just so I could go out and not see people whom I've either directly or indirectly insulted."

———

That night I visited my old housemate Anne. She'd married Michael, had two boys, and now lived in a new subdivision along the railroad tracks. We sat in her front room with a roaring fire and watched her older son put puzzles together on the floor. In her usual offhand and slightly amused way, she filled me in on everything I'd missed, which was "not much." Her brother Pat still lived at home; our old housemates had all moved away and married; the owner of the house had returned from England, renovated the place, and now spent his time in pubs reading his poetry to whoever would listen.

"Some new girls moved in there for a while before he came back, and apparently they were an awful shower of bitches."

Anne still worked at the ribbon factory—"till I die"— where rumors of its closing lingered on.

I asked her if she'd ever located her birth mother.

"I hounded the nuns," she said. "They kept putting me off and this kind of craic, but I kept hounding and ringing them. Eventually they rang me and asked me to come out. They said, 'Yes, we found your mother. She lives in Dublin and she's married, has no kids, and is very well off, but her husband doesn't know about you, and she doesn't want to meet you.'" She paused to reach over and hand her son a puzzle piece. "I said fair enough. I just wanted to know like." She got up and retrieved a glass of Guinness for me, saying as she handed it to me, "Happy . . . Hanukkah, is it?"

———

The ditches were deep with snow one day, and snowflakes shone like sequins in the sun over the river when I walked out into the country. From a hill, town lights glimmered below in hazy bands, and farther out, farm lights formed small uneven horizons across the valley. As I stood among some ancient abbey ruins, I remembered that long ago tenants of Roscrea worked the land of a man they called the Lord of the Soil, a designation for this absentee landlord that by its grandeur mocked him. As a place with more departures than arrivals, Roscrea still seemed like an unreconciled part of the world. But, as it was modernizing along with the rest of the country, its young might find more reasons to stay; and its emigrants might return sooner, bringing with them certain political, artistic, and cultural demands. I could already see the new "American" touches here and there, but, for now, Roscrea and its people seemed largely the same as when I left them. When Sarah returned here after decades away, the changes were much more dramatic, so much so that she said if she could have forecast the improvements she saw—paved roads, electricity, clothing stores—she never would have left.

The wintry silence was broken only by the sounds of cows stomping and snorting in the frozen dirt as seasons merged: yellow tussocks breaking through the snow; sea-green lichen encasing tree branches; and the scent of fox urine hanging over woodland paths.

As I headed back to town, I came across a flock of sheep blocking the road, roaming back and forth between the road's ivied walls.

"If it wouldn't trouble you none," the farmer said, asking me for help in steering them straight. His daughter used to help him "turn the sheep down for the night," he said, but she now lived in Australia.

The sky was deep blue and pink at the western horizon, the air sterling cold, and dogs howled as we passed. As the moon rose brightly, casting the snowy fields in a delft white light, I remembered one thing Billie had told me: "If there was life on Mars, sure it couldn't be more different than here is from New York."

Midweek I walked up the convent hill in a thin, bright rain, comforted by the lack of dramatic change here but aware that not everyone would be. I'd been told that the only movement the Mahoney Traveling family had made in the last few years was across town to a "holding site," a series of small houses, each not much larger than a camper, hidden away in a walled cul-de-sac. This was in keeping with a trend among Travelers in which they'd begun organizing or letting themselves be organized in order to maintain their culture, which in itself seemed to contradict the very culture they hoped to preserve.

Sheila ran out and greeted me in the rain when I arrived, chatting away as if I'd only been gone a day; she looked less distracted than I remembered but more troubled.

"I was very sick with nerves," she said, her voice a scratchy whisper, "and we're after having a lot of tragedies in the family this last month. Young boy hung himself, another killed with a car."

Inside the tiny house, Jimmy, who now sported a spiked bracelet and gold earring, sat in a corner humming to himself, and a teenage son stood in the bedroom doorway, "love" and "you" tattooed across his fingers. Boxing trophies and brass horse tackling lined a mantel below two conspicuous portraits of Jesus Christ and John Bon Jovi.

"You always had me in mind, did you?" Sheila asked as she handed me a cup of tea, a granddaughter clinging to her leg. When the girl began crying she picked her up. "What'll I do with a redhead?" She told me about Breda, the tomboy who'd often shadowed me from the bushes and who'd since married. "Godalmighty," Sheila proclaimed, "she used to be a nutcase."

As I wrote my address so Sheila could write to me, Jimmy leaned over my shoulder with curiosity.

"Brooklyn a fierce rough place," he told me, then sat back and continued humming to himself, staring ahead as if he could see through the wall in front of him.

Sheila and I talked a little more about her children, then she walked me outside. Before I left she held my arms down as if she expected me to fly off and gravely asked me something that clearly had been preying on her mind: "Do you feel Roscrea strange?"

———

I'd been having midday meals with my cousin Maureen. On my last day she handed me several obituaries and memorial cards, as if death was the only change I really needed to understand. It was a gloomy Sunday morning. I'd been sitting by the fire drowsily listening to an opera on the radio and watching orange sparks fly up in the darkness of the room as she piled more turf into it. We'd just returned from mass, where the church had smelled of fresh paint and the sermon had been as indecipherable as ever, "liberalism" and "confusion" being the only two words I was able to catch.

We discussed two as yet intangible changes that had occurred in Ireland: the legalization of divorce and the scandals plaguing the church. "They're hilarious," Maureen said of the "fallen" clergy, "the lot of them."

After a supper of stew and sherry, Maureen's sister Margaret rushed over from across the street. "There's a Siberian wind coming this way," she warned us, tugging at her sleeves and speaking with considerable authority. " 'Twill be perishing cold but the snow'll barely land."

Maureen gave her a doubtful smirk, then told me that one night a few years ago light drifts of Saharan sand had descended on Roscrea. "We didn't know what to think," she added, giving her hair a little pat.

Embers burst in the fire and flatbed trucks rumbled by outside as if in prelude to the storm. I sat up, completely awake now and thinking about winds that blow acres of the Great Desert across the planet, transforming the soil of drought in one place into rain forest somewhere else, and knowing that from then on I'd always think of white sand— and not rain—falling across Roscrea.